An Improbable Life

by

David C. Wilcox

About the Cover: The top photo shows the New Castle County Correctional Institution in Wilmington, Delaware and the bottom photo shows a California Institute of Technology walkway adjacent to the Millikan Library.

An Improbable Life

First edition copyright © 2007 by DCW Industries. All rights reserved.

First Printing: June, 2007

No part of this book may be reproduced or transmitted in any form or by any means, electronic or mechanical, including photocopying, recording, or any information storage and retrieval system, without permission in writing from

DCW Industries, Inc.
http://www.dcwindustries.com

This book was prepared with LaTeX as implemented by Personal TeX, Inc. of Mill Valley, California. It was printed and bound in the United States of America by Birmingham Press, Inc., San Diego, California.

Library of Congress Cataloging in Publication Data

Wilcox, David C.
    An Improbable Life
    1. Autobiography.
    2. Politics.
Library of Congress Control Number 2006910929

ISBN   978-1-928729-50-1 (1-928729-50-9)

Dedicated to

Jean Kane Foulke du Pont

About the Author

Dr. David C. Wilcox was born in Wilmington, Delaware. He was educated as an aeronautical engineer at two of the world's finest universities, the Massachusetts Institute of Technology (BS 1966) and the California Institute of Technology (PhD 1970). After spending the early part of his career with several Southern California aerospace companies, in 1973, he founded DCW Industries, Inc., a La Cañada, California firm for which he is currently President. He has taught several aerospace and mechanical engineering courses at both USC and UCLA.

His publications include more than 70 scientific papers and articles in some of the world's top aerospace engineering journals. He has published numerous scientific textbooks that are in use at universities worldwide. He has also written and published two political books advocating individual liberty and self reliance that are frequently quoted on the Internet.

Dr. Wilcox, whose ancestors came to America in 1630, is a descendent of the Wilcox and Landon families. His third great grandfather, Laban Landon, served as one of George Washington's bodyguards and produced a second great grandson, Alf Landon, who ran for President of the United States in 1936. His great grandfather, Sevellon Wilcox, fought with the Union army in the Civil War and was wounded at the Battle of Fredericksburg.

Since his first exposure to politics in the 1964 presidential election, Dr. Wilcox has advocated the conservative/libertarian ideas popularized by Barry Goldwater. He was a Republican primary candidate for the California State Assembly in 2004.

Contents

	Prologue	1
1	Shadows of the Past	3
2	Dad	9
3	Tragedy	33
4	Destruction	49
5	Redemption	81
6	Hope	95
7	The Bright Sun of Tomorrow	111
	Epilogue	125

Prologue

> *All things which humans hold sacred can only come from difficulty, struggle, and the growing idealization of bliss and perfection, which can only flourish in the mind when paradise is utterly lost.* – Aristotle

I offer this book with great humility. I do not assume that my achievements in life warrant interest from anyone but those who know me, and that consideration alone made me reluctant to write an entire book about myself.

There is a part of my life's story that friends and colleagues have assured me is interesting enough to write about. After all, they have told me, not too many people go from being a high-school dropout sitting in a prison cell to a Caltech PhD in less than a decade.

I have chosen to relate this part of my life because it has already served as a source of hope, and perhaps even inspiration, for many young people who have gotten off to a bad start in life. This book is intended to help such people and their loved ones. I offer the story of my troubled youth and how I survived it as an example of why young Americans should never give up on themselves.

Some of the events in this book happened more than a half century ago, and my memory is a bit foggy on some of the details.

Consequently, I have done careful research to help insure that all of the events and facts in this manuscript are true and occurred as described.

I want to thank my son, Robert, my brother, Robert, and six of my friends, Peter Bradshaw, Gregory Francis, Paul Hackett, Deborah Johannes, Sheila Voost Machuca and William Watts for thoughtful reviews of the manuscript as I prepared it. Maureen Milford of the News Journal in Wilmington, Delaware provided invaluable historical information about Wilmington in the 1950s and 1960s that greatly enhanced the manuscript's accuracy. I am especially grateful to Alcoholics Anonymous of Wilmington, Delaware for excellent research and valuable historical information about my father's involvement with AA in the 1940s and 1950s.

David C. Wilcox

Chapter 1

Shadows of the Past

Never suppose that in any possible situation, or under any circumstances, it is best for you to do a dishonorable thing. – Thomas Jefferson

"Please God, don't let them hear me breathing."

My lungs were on fire. I was breathing so hard — gasping for the cold night air. I was really scared. It seemed like one of the apartment managers had opened his apartment door almost at the same instant the rock had shattered the window. Before I even started running I could hear heavy footsteps dangerously close to the building's entrance. As I turned the corner of the building I heard the entrance door open and one of the men yelling.

"You little son of a bitch, wait until I get my hands on you!"

I ran as fast as my legs would carry me. I knew both managers were chasing me because I heard each of them screaming. I had to find a place to hide. These guys were big and mean. I was sure they wouldn't hesitate to hit me if they caught me.

I ducked into a building next to the street because I knew they would overtake me if I continued running much farther. If there had been more time to make my getaway, I would have run to the building farther from the street where I had left my bike. I smashed the light bulb on the lower level and wedged myself into a corner. Since my clothes were dark, it would be hard for the management guys to see me — well, as long as they didn't have a flashlight.

"Oh God, please don't let them have a flashlight."

If they didn't hear my breathing, surely they would hear my heartbeat. The pounding in my ears seemed as loud as the back beat on an Elvis Presley record. I could feel the veins pulsing so hard in my neck that they seemed to be on the brink of bursting. The thrill of getting revenge on these guys had been quickly replaced by fear — fear of being caught, fear of getting beat up and fear of having to explain it to Mom.

"God, I won't get in any more trouble if you'll just give me a break this time."

It was late November 1956. I had chosen refuge in one of the sixty-eight garden-style apartment buildings that made up Clifton Park Manor, a large development northeast of Wilmington, Delaware. Each building looked like an Army barracks, except for the red-brick construction. They were three-story buildings. To reach the bottom level you had to descend a short stairway. That's where I was hiding.

Although it had been a very mild autumn and the first snowfall had not yet arrived, it was nevertheless a chilly night. To make things worse I was sweating from running so hard. My clothes were moist and, as they began to dry, it made me even colder. I was starting to shiver as I huddled in that corner, hoping and praying that the apartment managers wouldn't find me. If I sat there much longer, I worried, even after my breathing and heart rate returned to normal, my chattering teeth might tip them off to where I was.

CHAPTER 1. SHADOWS OF THE PAST

I could just make out the door from beneath the stairwell. Suddenly the door opened and one of the managers reached for the light switch. The hair stood up on the back of my neck.

"They're so close now, and there's no way out," I thought, "and they're going to beat the crap out of me." I felt like I was going to throw up.

"The little bastard," thundered the other manager, "I'll bet it was one of those little creeps that skidded their bikes through the flower beds today."

"Dollars to donuts it was the kid on the bike I kicked," replied the manager who was groping for the switch in the dark. He didn't have a flashlight. "Oh hell, the light must be burned out down there — I can't see a thing."

"Forget it, he would've headed away from the street to stay out of the light. We better go back and cover that window, it's going to be pretty cold tonight."

The door closed. Thanks to a little dumb luck I had been spared discovery. But, I realized, I still had a problem to deal with. I would have to figure out how to fix the bent spokes on my bike's back wheel. Unless I could straighten them, I would need a new wheel, and Mom didn't have any money to spare.

"Thanks God," I whispered. I assumed my prayers had been answered and I would do my best to honor my promise to stay out of trouble. It hadn't occured to me that a just God would not make a bargain to protect me in a situation like this.

"I wonder if there's a bicycle store in the Mart," I thought as I waited until it was safe to come out of my hiding spot. "If there is maybe they can tell me how to fix the spokes."

Clifton Park Manor was located on a hill overlooking the Merchandise Mart. It was a 500,000-square-foot shopping center on the west side of Governor Printz Boulevard, centered around the

Strawbridge and Clothier store, one of the first department stores in Delaware. Opened in 1952, the Merchandise Mart was the state's first regional shopping complex. A group of prominent businessmen, many of whom were officers of the DuPont Company, developed the Merchandise Mart and Clifton Park Manner in America's post World War II building boom. The DuPont Edge Moor plant was located just east of Governor Printz Boulevard, and the company steered many of the young professionals who were moving to Wilmington into the communities northeast of the city.

Consequently, many of the families living in Clifton Park Manor and the immediate vicinity were employed by either the DuPont Company or the Hercules Powder Company, which had been part of DuPont. It was a prosperous area and, in those days, parking spaces in the Merchandise Mart were very hard to find during the holidays. After demographic changes, Clifton Park Manor (now called Paladin Club) would eventually become a haven for drugs and crime. Robberies, vandalism and muggings became routine events in the shopping center and merchants moved out. Today, the Merchandise Mart — renamed as Merchants Square — has the appearance of a blighted area whose days of prosperity have long since faded.

But in 1956 it was an exciting place to go. Just after the presidential election in early November, I had seen the glee on the faces of a group that had gone to a restaurant in the Merchandise Mart to celebrate the re-election of President Eisenhower. Everybody seemed to like the president, and that included Mom and Dad.

"After all those years of Roosevelt and Truman," Mom said after his election in 1952, "it's wonderful to have a good man as president again." Dad smiled quietly and said, "Indeed it is."

CHAPTER 1. SHADOWS OF THE PAST

On the eighth of October I had stood outside one of the stores in the Merchandise Mart and watched the fifth game of the 1956 World Series between the Brooklyn Dodgers and the New York Yankees. I had seen the final out of the game on the store's TV screen — Don Larsen, whose career was otherwise undistinguished, had just pitched a perfect game. It made me happy that I had witnessed an ordinary man doing something great.

However, there were many things that made me unhappy in 1956. We had moved from the neighborhood in Richardson Park southwest of Wilmington where I had lived all of my young life. We had gone from being reasonably well to do to just barely making ends meet. Along with all of my childhood friends, I had lost my best friend in the world. The worst thing of all was that I had found out everything I believed in was based on lies — lies my best friend in the world told me.

Nothing made sense any more without my best friend. He had taught me so much about math and a code of values that would eventually guide my life. But, none of that mattered now.

"Why should I follow the rules when the rule makers don't? My friends don't care about the rules and they're real people. They don't lie to me and I don't lie to them. We trust each other. My friends are solid like oaks! Well, all except my best friend."

I still hadn't gotten over the betrayal by the person who was my best friend in the world, the person I looked up to with love and respect, the person who was my first great teacher — MY DAD. It made me want to scream, but I just stayed silent.

"Mom is right," I thought, "Dad *is* a liar. That's why they got a divorce. It really doesn't matter though 'cause I'll be thirteen in a few weeks. I don't need a mother or a father telling me what to do anyway. I'm old enough to take charge of my life from now on."

I stood up, kicked the wall in anger and lit a cigarette. It had been about ten minutes since the apartment managers had gone, so I decided that it was safe to make my way home.

I got my bike and started pedaling up the hill to Bellefonte. My back wheel wobbled a lot and it took a great deal of effort to pedal. About two-thirds of the way home I had to stop and rest. Lighting another cigarette I thought, "In five more years I'll graduate from high school and then I can go anywhere I want — no matter what anybody says." I had always thought that when I finished school I would go to work for Dad. That didn't seem very likely now that he had left me.

I was angry with him, yet I thought about him constantly. He had rarely spoken to me about what his life had been like before I was born, nor had Mom. I'm sure she would have told me about their life together if I had asked, but my tangled emotions stood in the way of asking. Unsurprisingly, as a twelve-year-old boy, I had no idea of how intertwined my fate was with Dad's.

Chapter 2

Dad

Of all the properties which belong to honorable men, not one is so highly prized as that of character. – Henry Clay

Dad's full name was Robert Landon Wilcox. He was born on February 25, 1903, a little less than ten months before Orville and Wilbur Wright would make the first-ever powered flight of a heavier-than-air craft. Dad told me he was proud that he was born in 1903 because of the Wright brothers' achievement in Kitty Hawk, North Carolina.

He was the third of four children, three of whom were boys and one a girl. His grandfather, Sevellon Wilcox, was a Civil War veteran who included a statement in his will that he was a Republican. That he was proud of having been an abolitionist — which Republicans of that era were — seems the most logical explanation of why he included such a fact in his will. After all, the Wilcox family arrived in America in 1630 and consisted of a long line of farmers and preachers. Many of the preachers of the Civil War era carried the abolitionist banner and played a critical role in bringing an end to slavery in America.

Figure 2.1: *The Wilcox Family in 1911. Seated (from left to right): Uncle Arthur, Dad, Grandma Mary. Standing (from left to right): Uncle Stanley, Grandpa Cory Ell, Aunt Mabel.*

Dad's older brother, Arthur, was a natural-born farmer who would eventually take over the family farm. His older sister, Mabel, was destined to become a school teacher. His younger brother, Stanley, was interested in rapidly developing twentieth-century innovations, especially automobiles. In addition to encouraging Dad's fascination with modern technology, his father, Cory Ell Wilcox, made sure his son was tough enough to face the world by having wrestling matches in the front yard with his brothers and, sometimes, with other boys from neighboring farms.

CHAPTER 2. DAD

Dad's mother, Mary, was a descendent of the Landon family, which had arrived in America about the same time as the Wilcox family. Her great grandfather, Laban Landon, served as one of George Washington's bodyguards. He was selected, as were all of Washington's bodyguards, because he "neither smoked nor drank and was of the highest moral character." One of Laban Landon's descendents was Alf Landon who ran for President against Franklin Roosevelt in 1936.

When Dad was born, the Wilcox family lived in the town of LeRoy, Pennsylvania, which lies in the "Endless Mountains" near the northern border with New York. LeRoy was, and still is, a farming community. Dad had a marvelous sense of humor and often pointed out that in his day, "the Wilcox's were the dirt farmers and the Landons owned the general store." When I visited LeRoy in the mid 1990s, I found that not a whole lot had changed in the area. There were still a lot of Wilcox and Landon descendents living there. The Wilcox's are now dairy farmers *and the Landons still own the general store!*

Dad lamented that, having arrived in America not too long after the Pilgrims landed at Plymouth Rock, the family should have become rich landowners. "But," he said, "my ancestors chose to live in caves." That's how Dad described the Endless Mountains, which he always thought made an odd place to set up a farm.

The family indeed found it difficult to make a living by farming in LeRoy and looked southward for a better life. When Dad was seven, the family moved first to Trumbauersville and ultimately to Quakertown. Both of these small towns are near the southeast corner of Pennsylvania about fifty miles north of Philadelphia. Originally named the "Great Swamp," Quakertown played a notable role in the Revolutionary War. The Liberty Bell was concealed in Quakertown, behind what is now called Liberty Hall, on its way to its hiding place in the Lehigh Valley to protect it from the British during America's struggle for independence.

Independence Day was one of the big events for Dad and his younger brother, Stanley. They were notorious pranksters and every year, on the Fourth of July, they would carefully assemble what amounted to a pipe bomb that they placed in a meadow about 1,000 feet from the farm's barn. When they ignited it, according to one of my Uncle Arthur's sons, Ralph Wilcox, "the blast was so loud that it could be heard all over Bucks County." Coming from a family with veterans of both the Revolutionary and Civil Wars, it is clear that they wanted to share their patriotism with everyone. And, I'm sure they "reasoned," what better way was there than to create a blast loud enough to scare horses, cows, dogs and, probably, everything else that breathed?

While the Wilcox family prospered in its new location, Dad didn't like farming. He was exceptionally talented in mathematics and his passion for science was an obsession. He was acutely aware of the tremendous changes that were reshaping the world at the dawn of the twentieth century. Automobiles and airplanes had made it possible for people to travel to destinations far beyond the immediate countryside. Henry Ford was building cars on his assembly line in ninety-three minutes. Navy Lieutenant Commander Albert C. Read made the first successful flight across the Atlantic from Newfoundland to England with stops at the Azores and Portugal in 1919. Medical advances had extended the life expectancy of white males in America from forty-eight years in 1900 to fifty-six years in 1920. Thomas Edison's inventions had demonstrated the wonders of electricity, whose theoretical foundations had been established by James Clerk Maxwell near the end of the Civil War.

CHAPTER 2. DAD

When Dad graduated from high school in 1921, he was especially fascinated with radio. This brand new mass communications medium was just starting to take off and was dramatically altering communication all over the globe. Building a radio from parts purchased from a local supplier, scrounged, mail ordered, and carefully assembled was the intellectual challenge for the "techy" of this era, much as personal computers were in the late 1970s and through the 1980s. During the rapidly developing radio-design period in the 1920s, radios were obsolete in three to six months after they hit the shelves. Technology was changing that fast!

It's extremely likely that Dad was one of the "techies" who had a radio in 1921. The most common amateur radio of the era used a lead galena crystal with a device called a cat whisker to find the signal. The parts cost all of $6.00 — earphones would have been extra. With an outdoors antenna, he would have been able to hear broadcasts from towns within a hundred miles or so and, if their signal was strong, from even farther away.

I remember Dad telling me Pittsburgh radio station KDKA was one of the very first and one of the most powerful from its very beginnings. In late 1920 the station increased its power from 100 Watts to 500 Watts, and people as far away as Washington DC could pick up KDKA broadcasts. He certainly would have been able to hear them on the Wilcox-family farm in Quakertown, Pennsylvania on a clear day.

And it was clear that an eighteen-year-old boy with a strong aptitude for mathematics in 1921 would find the attraction of the tremendous changes brought about by science to be compelling. Dad was swept off of the farm by the tidal wave of advancing technology. Armed with a brilliant mind and tons of ambition, he headed south to Philadelphia to continue his education.

With a population of just over 1.8 million in 1921, Philadelphia was America's third largest city — only New York City and Chicago were larger. It had served as the original seat of American government until December 1, 1800 when the District of Columbia became the nation's capital. In addition to its historical importance to the nation, it was a thriving metropolis with top-notch educational institutions such as Temple University, La Salle College and Thomas Jefferson University. Dad would eventually study calculus and physics at Temple.

His objective was to learn everything he could about the science and technology of radio. The school he selected was the Philadelphia Wireless Technical Institute. Although details of his time in Philadelphia are sketchy, he clearly accomplished his goal of mastering radio. He eventually earned the reputation of being such a genius when it came to radio that, according to my Aunt Isabel (my mother's younger sister), "if your radio wasn't working, when he walked into the room and snapped his fingers it came to life."

Dad worked at a radio station in Philadelphia and soon became enamored with a petite woman who played piano and sang as part of a broadcast. The young woman, four years older than Dad, was Helen Mae Miller. Born in Wilmington, Delaware on February 27, 1899, she had come to Philadelphia for an opportunity to perform on radio.

Helen was the second of William Clinton Miller's three daughters — her older sister's name was Violet and her younger sister was Emma Isabel. Actually, her father, a printer by trade, was originally named William Oscar Miller but so disliked his middle name that he legally changed it to Clinton. He selected his new middle name in honor of deWitt Clinton, who played an important

CHAPTER 2. DAD

role in building the Erie Canal during the nineteenth century. The Miller family had very early roots in America, which included Abraham Miller who served under George Washington during the Revolutionary War.

Figure 2.2: *Mom in 1923.*

Mom and Dad married on September 8, 1923, and a little more than a year later their first child, Elizabeth Elinor, was born. Times were good for the brand-new Wilcox family. Mom told me that her favorite presidents had been Warren Harding and Calvin Coolidge. I can understand why since the decade of the 1920s would see Harding and Coolidge reduce the maximum income tax rate from 73% to 24%, which helped fuel the "Roaring Twenties." This period of rapid industrial growth accelerated America's development into a world class economic power whose prosperity was unrivaled anywhere on the planet.

With a solid education under his belt, Dad and his family headed south to Wilmington, Delaware, an industrial city that was a microcosm of America's economic might.

In comparison to Quakertown, Wilmington was a big city. Between the Civil War and World War I, Wilmington had grown from a population of just over 20,000 people to a booming east-coast industrial city of 110,000. The Civil War had a profound effect on the city's economy. While Delaware was officially a Union state, its southern counties were loyal to the Confederacy. Delaware's northern partisans were centered in Wilmington, which lies north of the famous Mason-Dixon line, the boundary between Union and Confederate states. By 1868, Wilmington was producing more iron ships than the rest of the United States combined and, thanks to the Wilmington-based DuPont Chemical Company, was first in the production of gunpowder.

Census records of 1930 show that Dad and his family had taken up residence in Wilmington by that time. On September 22, 1930 the family expanded its size to four. This child was a son who would bear Dad's name, Robert Landon Wilcox, Jr. Wilmington had a bustling market for Dad's skills and he worked as a radio repairman. However, like most Americans, his success was jeopardized by another market that had just come to a screeching halt.

In response to the 1929 collapse of the stock market, which signaled the coming of the Great Depression, President Herbert Hoover increased the maximum tax rate from 24% to 63% in an attempt to increase the amount of money in the public treasury. His move did not work and caused federal tax collections to fall by one half! This simultaneously crippled the government's efforts to provide relief for the most desperate families and further worsened America's business climate.

What might have been a severe, but relatively short, recession turned into one of the times of greatest misery and suffering

CHAPTER 2. DAD

in America's history. One of every four workers would be unable to find work and thousands of factories stood idle. The most powerful and productive industrial nation the world has ever known was at a standstill.

Dad and his fellow Americans suffered because of two major blunders by America's government that doomed millions to more than a decade of hardship. As Economist Milton Friedman would explain several decades later, the first was failure of the Federal Reserve to regulate the country's supply of money in a way that would encourage investment and expansion of business. This brand new agency had key personnel in both New York City and Washington DC. It had been created to fill the void left by recently retired, legendary banker J. P. Morgan, who had coordinated America's banking industry without government interference for several decades. The groups in these two cities were engaged in a "turf war" to determine who would control the Federal Reserve. It was not their love of humanity that guided these political appointees' actions, and America's well being was put on hold. One consequence was that loans from banks to businesses were extremely difficult to obtain — the opposite of what was needed to pull America's economy out of its slump.

Dad was probably very aware of the second blunder, which was made by the United States Congress. In a move to "protect American jobs from foreign competition," Congress passed the Hawley-Smoot tariff law of 1930 that raised tariffs to the highest level ever on virtually all imports to the United States. Since tariffs are taxes, they were attempting to tax the country back to prosperity. It didn't work. Not only did America continue losing jobs to less expensive overseas business competitors, the Halley-Smoot law triggered retaliatory action from abroad. The net result was that America, in effect, exported the Great Depression to the rest of the world. Congress may have acted in good faith but certainly not on good economic theory.

Just before the 1932 presidential election, Dad's father Cory Ell passed away. In his will he specified that the family farm be divided evenly among his four children. However, only his oldest son Arthur had an interest in farming. Mabel had married and would soon move to Detroit, Stanley had plans of moving to California and Dad had been gone from the farm for a decade. Arthur bought the shares of his sister and brothers for approximately $5,000 — enough to buy eight brand-new cars in 1932. Dad used his share of the money to set up a radio repair and sales business in Wilmington, located near Eighth and Madison Streets.

Franklin Roosevelt defeated Herbert Hoover in the 1932 election. Blaming the Great Depression on the "failure of capitalism," Roosevelt promised reform through his "New Deal" — programs and laws that would dramatically expand the role of the government's regulation and control of business. Some of his proposed laws would have given the president powers that were prohibited by the United States Constitution, and the Supreme Court struck them down. Frustrated by the Court, Roosevelt even tried to change the U. S. Constitution by increasing the number of Supreme Court justices. He wanted to pack it with judges who would rule in his favor. He was unsuccessful in this attempt to undermine the balance of power in America's government.

Because of these actions, Dad didn't like the new president and said, "Franklin Roosevelt is the closest thing to a dictator that America's ever had."

Roosevelt's New Deal did little to cure America's economic woes — the dreadful effects of the Federal Reserve battle and the misguided Hawley-Smoot law could not be overcome by any actions the President might have taken. The Great Depression persisted with jobs being scarce and with millions standing in lines all across the continent waiting for a government-supplied bowl of soup.

To help enhance his career, Dad attended night courses at Temple University from 1934 through 1937. His studies included three semesters of calculus and one semester of physics. This provided tools he could use to analyze and design advanced electrical circuits. One of his earliest designs was a lighting system that changed colors and could be used in store-front windows. Experimenting with television in its infancy, Dad was certainly on top of his profession, keeping pace with modern developments.

Dad also designed machines for winding copper wire about a cylinder, creating an important electronic circuit element known as an induction coil — or coil for short. This opened new horizons for the business, and he concentrated on manufacturing coils for model airplanes. He named his evolving business the Wilmington Coil Company.

In 1936 the family adopted a large brown and white beagle. Betty (my sister Elizabeth's nickname) had a boyfriend named Joe and she insisted that the dog bear his name. Dad couldn't say no to his daughter, but there was one problem — Joe was a female. So, he named her Josephine, and her nickname was Joe. Dad and Joe got along wonderfully. She had a remarkable sense of time and, every evening at about 4:30, she would take up a spot near the front door in preparation for Dad's return from work.

The Republican Party selected Alf Landon as its 1936 presidential candidate. He and Dad were both direct descendents of Laban Landon, which meant they were cousins — sixth cousins to be precise. "That's my cousin running for president," Dad boasted during the election campaign. Despite his abysmal record in getting America's economy moving and Landon's charges of widespread corruption in his administration, Roosevelt prevailed in the 1936 election, winning with more than 60% of the vote.

One reason for Roosevelt's popularity was the fact that, during his first term in office, America ended prohibition. Roosevelt favored an end to prohibition so it was a promise he kept. Brewing and selling alcoholic beverages was no longer illegal. The experiment with enforcing an unenforceable law and the crime and corruption that attended prohibition had finally ended. Americans could now go out and "have a beer with the boys" without concealing what they were doing from the police. For millions, it was a relief.

Dad enjoyed having a beer with the boys and even added a new dimension to the concept. One evening, Betty noticed with alarm that Joe was missing. Mom decided to go out and look for her. After searching the immediate neighborhood, she eventually came upon one of Dad's favorite bars. And there sat Joe on a bar stool next to Dad. She was wearing his tie and drinking beer out of an ashtray.

On another occasion, poor Joe came home after an evening out with Dad and she was totally pie eyed. Dad's explanation was one of the tall tales he was famous for. He claimed she had come upon a rock filled with beer and drank it.

But, as the years wore on, the humor in Dad's drinking escapades wore off. There were too many evenings that the family would sit up late wondering if he was okay and fretting about when he would finally return home. Money was not that plentiful and Dad was spending too much of his earnings at his favorite "watering holes." For Dad, the end of prohibition had unleashed a weakness that would get in the way of his happiness in both his professional and his private life. As the Great Depression deepened so did Dad's immersion in booze. Dad was an alcoholic.

CHAPTER 2. DAD

——— • ———

"Yesterday, December 7, 1941 — a date which will live in infamy — the United States of America was suddenly and deliberately attacked by naval and air forces of the Empire of Japan."

So began President Roosevelt as he addressed the United States Congress requesting a declaration of war on Japan for its attack on Pearl Harbor. His speech was carried all over the world by radio. Many years later, virtually every American who heard the announcement on December 7, 1941 could tell you where he or she was. It was as stunning and ominous as the news of the terrorist attacks sixty years later on September 11, 2001.

It is the speech that Roosevelt is best remembered for, and it transcended partisan politics. America had been deceived by Japanese diplomats who, for many weeks, had stressed that peace in the Pacific was possible. All the while, as they deliberately lied, the Japanese military planned a massive attack on Pearl Harbor in Hawaii. The object of the attack was to cripple America's Navy. Without warning, the Japanese launched a bombing attack that either sunk or disabled most of the U. S. ships docked in Pearl Harbor early on a Sunday morning. They killed 3,000 American servicemen in the course of the attack — about the same number of defenseless civilians who died in the terrorist attacks of "9/11."

In what was probably his finest hour, President Roosevelt united all Americans in a quest to introduce the devious and deadly Japanese rulers to the concept of justice. The declaration of war would eventually include Japan's allies, Italy and Germany. Both countries had declared war on the United States immediately following the Pearl Harbor attack. Roosevelt promised in his speech that, "With confidence in our armed forces — with the unbounded determination of our people — we will gain the inevitable triumph — so help us God."

Americans rallied to the cause. Patriotism permeated every level of society, from famous people to dishwashers, from wealthy to poor, from college graduate to grade-school dropout. Many Hall of Fame baseball stars including Joe DiMaggio, Bob Feller, Warren Spahn and Ted Williams sacrificed prime years of their careers to fight for America. It was common for Hollywood stars like Charles Bronson, Clark Gable, Charlton Heston, George C. Scott and James Stewart to join the ranks of the military.

Three of my Uncle Arthur's sons served in the armed forces. His eldest, Sevellon, joined the Army and his younger, Frank, was a Marine who fought in the Guadalcanal campaign. Lasting from August 1942 to February 1943, it was the first significant victory by Allied forces over Japanese troops in the Pacific. The Guadalcanal Campaign was a major blow to the Japanese and a key turning point in World War II. After the battle, America and its allies shifted from defensive operations to offensive while Japan — for the first time in the war — was forced to focus much more on defense than on offense.

Arthur's youngest son, Ralph Wilcox, lied about his age so he could join the Navy when he was seventeen. He sailed on the *USS Steady*, a minesweeper that operated in the Mediterranean, assisting the war effort in Africa and Europe. His tour of duty lasted from 1942 to 1946. All three of Uncle Arthur's sons who served in the armed forces survived World War II.

By contrast, the war brought tragedy to my Aunt Isabel. Her husband, Warren Sergeant, had a dental practice on the Bataan Peninsula in the Philippines when Pearl Harbor was attacked. Prior to the battle for the island of Corregidor, Japan attacked the Bataan Peninsula. Uncle Warren was one of approximately 75,000 people taken prisoner by the Japanese after U. S. forces, who had run out of ammunition, surrendered in April of 1942.

CHAPTER 2. DAD

He survived the infamous Bataan Death March in which 10,000 Americans and Filipinos perished.

After more than two years in Prisoner of War (POW) Camps Bilibid and Santo Tomás, he was crowded onto Japanese "hell ship" *Arison Maru*. He was one of 1,790 Americans being transported to Japan where they would have been forced into slave labor. The ship sailed on October 10, 1944, just ten days before General MacArthur returned to the Philippines. In violation of international treaties, the Japanese did not mark the ship with red crosses, which would have indicated that American POWs were on board. Unaware of the POWs, on October 24, 1944, an American submarine torpedoed the *Arison Maru*, sending it to the bottom of the South China Sea. There were nine survivors. Uncle Warren was not one of them.

Since he would soon turn thirty-nine, Dad was too old to serve active duty and, at eleven, my brother Bob was too young. However, Dad found another way to contribute to the war effort. He had an idea for an assembly-line operation that started with the coil-winding machines he had designed and built. He made a proposal to the U. S. Army to manufacture coils for walkie-talkies, hand-held radio units that troops used to communicate during battles. The Army awarded him a substantial contract to manufacture the coils.

As part of the contract, Dad built a factory on the southwest side of Wilmington, located on Brookside Drive in Richardson Park. The factory was of standard eastern seaboard red-brick construction and proudly displayed its Wilmington Coil Company banner in front. In order to be closer to his business, Dad moved the family to 115 Grier Avenue, just off of Maryland Avenue, in Richardson Park. With this lucrative contract from the War Department, Dad had finally achieved real prosperity.

Dad's was one of thousands of factories that either sprung up or reopened after years of being idle as part of the war effort. Americans were finally going back to work. With the immediate need to build up America's ability to wage war against the ruthless Japanese Empire and the murderous Nazi regime of Adolf Hitler, the war ended the Great Depression.

Figure 2.3: *Wilmington Coil Company during World War II. Dad is seated in the second row near the center of the picture.*

As in many factories, Dad's employees were almost exclusively women. So many men were on their way to Europe to engage the Germans and Italians or to the Pacific Islands to fight the Japanese, that their wives and loved ones had to fill the suddenly abundant supply of jobs. As I wrote this book, it was my great pleasure to speak with Marguerite Griffith, one of Dad's employees during World War II. She described him as being well dressed, always wearing a suit and tie. She also said he was a

CHAPTER 2. DAD

wonderful man to work for. Although she knew he did a lot of drinking, there was never any sign of his problem with alcohol in the workplace. "All of the women who worked at Wilmington Coil Company loved him," she told me, "and we did a lot of singing while we worked."

His penchant for practical jokes was legendary at home. One day he wired my brother's bed. When Bob climbed between the blankets, his body was suddenly tickled by an electric current. He knew instantly who was responsible because of Dad's loud "Har-har-har" that was probably heard by the next-door neighbors. On another evening, he had a little fun at the expense of my sister Betty. Knowing she had the odd habit of brushing her teeth in the dark, he strategically placed a tube of shaving cream in the bathroom. Dad and my brother shared a laugh as they listened to Betty spitting out the foul-tasting substitute for her toothpaste.

Despite his affection and love for his family, the bad effects of Dad's drinking were always there. There were weekend binges that superseded family outings. And all of this was taking a terrible toll on his wife. Mom had been a happy-go-lucky lady when they had married. Those days had been washed away by the raging current of alcohol that was numbing not only his mind, but his relationship with his family as well.

In 1942, when she was just eighteen, Betty married. She would confide to me many years later that, although she loved Dad dearly, a big part of her decision to marry so young was to escape the insanity of life with him.

―――― • ――――

Mom spoke into the telephone barely believing her own words as she said, "Betty, I'm pregnant."

"Oh my God Mom, are you sure?" my sister replied.

"Yes, Doctor Squires confirmed it this morning. The baby will be born in January."

"Oh Lord, mine is due sometime in October."

It was probably June 1943 when Mom learned that her child-bearing years had not yet ended. Betty would soon be nineteen and no longer lived at home. Bob would be thirteen before year's end. The doctor had confirmed that sometime just before her forty-fifth birthday, she would give birth to her third child.

Neither Mom nor Dad ever discussed the matter with me, but it's hard to imagine that mine was a planned pregnancy. It was very uncommon for women of the era to have babies after they turned forty. Betty told me she had been embarrassed that Mom was pregnant at the same time she was.

Although the tide of World War II was beginning to turn in America's favor, there were critical battles both in the Pacific and in Europe that had yet to be fought. The high death tolls on Iwo Jima in February and March of 1945, for example, had not yet been suffered nor had the D-Day invasion of Normandy on June 6, 1944 been accomplished. Since World War II would not end until August 1945, I would be a "war baby."

Almost certainly, as 1943 wore on, Dad must have done a great deal of introspection, assessing what his life had amounted to. He had been married for twenty years, yet he had not achieved a warm and satisfying romantic relationship with his wife. Mom was very unhappy. She had become the bookkeeper for his business, for example, not from a desire to be by his side, but in defense of her family. She had taken control of the family finances to counter Dad's desire to have the very best clothes and automobiles while continuing to enhance the profitability of his favorite bars. They argued constantly about money and his drinking. The gravity of his addiction to alcohol and its effect on his

CHAPTER 2. DAD

relationship with his wife must have been weighing heavily on him.

Possibly, Betty's marrying and moving out almost immediately after graduating from high school helped him realize that something was missing in the Wilcox household. Increasingly, it was clear that Bob was closer to Mom than to him, and that it was because he was so often undependable. The glaring impossibility of being a good father and a drunk must have been a blinding reality more than at any other point in his life.

And what would his professional life be like after the war ended and the demand for walkie-talkie coils ceased? He was forty years old and the years of heavy drinking were beginning to show. He was graying at a relatively young age and the natural aches and pains of middle age were greeting him as he finished his workday. His mind was still sharp and he was surely confident that he had many productive years ahead of him. His career had just begun to soar, but the storm clouds of alcoholism could easily force him back onto the runway of life's might-have-beens.

But, these things had all been matters of concern for many years. What was different in 1943? The catalyst for all of his introspection and the dramatic change that was about to occur centered on one key question — what kind of family life would his third child have? Would his being a lovable prankster in between drunken binges be satisfactory? It hadn't been with his first two children. Would the constant bickering with his miserable and depressed wife provide a good home life for his new child? It hadn't done so for his first two children. Would a drop off in his career because too many dollars floated away in a sea of beer and cocktails rather than creating a rising tide in the business be helpful for the welfare of his new child? It hadn't helped his first two children.

All of my ability to reason tells me Dad considered all of these things as January 1944 approached. It could not have been otherwise because he was on the brink of making the most important change of his life.

——— • ———

"It's a boy," proclaimed Dr. Squires.

Wilmington General Hospital was two miles north of Richardson Park at the intersection of Linden and Broom Streets. The hospital complex was beautiful in the fall but, by January, most of the trees had shed their leaves as the winter chill engulfed the city. Our family doctor had been summoned to the hospital and delivered me to the world at 8:31 am on January 12, 1944.

Everything had happened on schedule. Betty had given birth to a daughter, Carole Hurschman, on October 29, 1943. This meant that I was younger than my niece! As we grew up, Carole was more like a sister to me than a niece, and she absolutely refused to call me Uncle. I'm sure it was a relief to Mom that her pregnancy had finally come to a conclusion.

Mom was a slender woman who stood five feet three inches and weighed not much over a hundred pounds. Her hair was beginning to gray, perhaps a bit early because of the stress and worry her marriage to Dad had brought to her. Blessed with a beautiful singing voice and a strong moral foundation, she loved her children dearly, including the little blonde-haired son she had just added to her family.

I can only guess about how Dad reacted, but it would have been very characteristic of him to gather some of the women working for him together. He may have told them that he had been studying the present alignment of the planets from Mercury all the way out to Pluto. He may well have gone on for ten to fifteen minutes explaining how the planets' gravitational fields influenced

CHAPTER 2. DAD

each other and, by contributing to shifts in the center of mass of the universe, would help cause solar flares that periodically appeared on the sun.

The long dissertation would probably have included a layman's explanation of how the planets' elliptical orbits differed from circular orbits and how this made their relative positions very interesting to analyze mathematically. All of this would have led up to him explaining how he had discovered that the sun was the brightest it had been in two centuries that day, that the North Star would be especially bright that evening and that, if they looked closely, they would see that the Moon's face would have a wink and a smile.

"Do you think this might have something to do with my son, David, being born today?" he would have asked after having everyone convinced that he was giving them a peek into the scientific wonders of the universe. I can imagine the laughter as the women realized they had been snookered by another one of his tall tales.

Dad didn't celebrate my birth that evening by having a few drinks. Rather, he probably thought about what he would say when he addressed a much more solemn group two days later, and he would not be trying to make them laugh. His mind was made up — he had summoned enough courage and determination to go through with his plan.

―――― • ――――

"I'm a God-damned genius, and you people have to save me!"

The man addressing the Alcoholics Anonymous (AA) meeting in downtown Wilmington stunned the crowd with his opening words. It was Thursday evening on January 14, 1944, and it was the first meeting of the newly formed Wilmington AA. Dad had decided to seek the help he so urgently needed. His audience observed that he was a sharp dresser and, as he continued speaking, he demonstrated a magnificent command of the English language. He was a muscular, barrel-chested man with a stylish mustache and graying hair who stood five feet six inches tall. His deep and penetrating eyes made it clear that he was a man of keen intellect.

As he spoke of his admission that he was an alcoholic and of how desperately he wanted to break free of his addiction, Dad brought tears to the eyes of many in the audience. He had delivered his plea in such eloquent terms that it was truly heart wrenching, especially the part about wanting to be the kind of father the boy who had been born just two days ago deserved.

One member of that audience was Hiram Warder, a lawyer who would soon become Dad's friend for life. Like Dad, he had a Pennsylvania ancestor who was involved with America's Founding Fathers, namely James Wilson who signed both the Declaration of Independence and the United States Constitution. As our family lawyer, Hiram would eventually have a profound effect on my life, although in a way that neither he nor Dad could have ever guessed on the evening of January 14, 1944. Dad never told me he quit drinking the day I was born. Hiram did, including a touching description of the attention-grabbing way Dad introduced himself to AA members two days after my birth.

Dad found his salvation at Alcoholics Anonymous. On the day of my birth, his healing began, and for all the rest of his days he never took another drink. In 1947 Dad insisted that Mom and Betty come to an AA meeting with him. It may have been triggered by the death of his older brother Arthur, who was only fifty-one. Arthur had suffered a massive heart attack. Plagued by high blood pressure, Dad may have viewed it as a warning that he should not delay in telling his family what was in his heart.

Figure 2.4: *Visiting the Wilcox family farm in 1947. From left to right: Uncle Arthur, Aunt Ruth, Dad, me and Mom. Arthur would suffer a fatal heart attack before the end of the year, which may have hastened Dad's need to repair his broken family.*

When the meeting began, Mom and Betty discovered that Dad was the featured speaker. As he spoke, he looked directly at both of them and apologized for all the years of pain and misery his drinking had brought to his two loved ones — such an apology constitutes Step Nine of the Alcoholics Anonymous Twelve-Step program. It was an emotion-packed expression of his love for them. The full extent of Dad's character was evident as he made his apology in a room filled with people rather than doing it privately. His second great grandfather, Laban Landon — who Dad may not have known had been selected as one of George Washington's bodyguards because he "neither smoked nor drank and was of the highest moral character" — surely would have been proud of his descendent on that evening.

Chapter 3

Tragedy

> *Whatever their future, at the dawn of their lives, men seek a noble vision of man's nature and of life's potential.* –
> Ayn Rand

The field behind Richardson Park School extends about 500 feet to the east and 400 feet from southern to northern sides. The portion of the field at the western end next to the school is the playground. There is a baseball field near the southeastern corner and a softball field at the northeastern corner. The layout today looks much the same as it looked in 1949.

One of my earliest and most vivid memories is of dejectedly peering out at that field when I was five. I was dejected because of an unreasonable "one-size-fits-all" decision by the school board. It was summertime and I recall the smell of freshly mowed grass that penetrated all the way across Grier Avenue, which is separated from the field by a single line of homes on the northern side of the field. When I learned of the school board's decision, I crossed the street and walked between two of the houses to the edge of the field. Very few houses had fences in those days and nobody complained about neighborhood children making a short trek across their lawn to go to the playground. When I reached the field, I lay down on my stomach, planted my elbows in the grass in front of me and propped my head up with my hands — I'm sure it was a perfect pose for a Norman Rockwell painting.

As usual, the field was bustling with activity from one end to the other. Big kids were playing a hardball game on the baseball diamond and younger kids were playing softball not too far from my vantage point. On the playground end I could make out a few families with their children. Some had laid blankets on the ground for a picnic — it was an era when families made time for family outings.

Staring out at the field I thought, "It's not fair, I know I can do good in first grade."

The school-district rules were very rigid. In order to enter first grade, you had to be six years old on December 31. Since I wouldn't be six until January 12, I would have to wait another year before I could start my education. I felt like I was being punished. Mom and Dad tried to convince them that I was ready, but school officials wouldn't budge.

"Dad said I know more about math than any other kid on the block — I don't wanna stay home."

My friends and I had climbed just about every tree in the field behind my house. We had built an underground fort at the end of Grier Avenue. We had begun construction of a submarine that we planned on using to explore a local pond, but quit the project when Dad said we would surely drown. If there had been a mountain, we would have climbed it. We had done just about everything pre-school-age kids could think of to do. It was time to move on to something new, something challenging. For most of my friends, that new frontier was school. But, for the sake of twelve days, I wouldn't be experiencing the adventure with them.

CHAPTER 3. TRAGEDY

I'm not sure when our evening ritual began, but it was certainly earlier than 1949 because I already knew a lot about numbers. Seeing my disappointment about not being able to start school, Dad reoriented our special time together from reading the newspaper comic strips to teaching me much more about math and improving my reading skills. We would set up shop in his bedroom where my first great teacher taught me my most important lesson — the joy of learning.

I already recognized all of the numbers and could count as high as I wanted. Thanks to Dad, when I finally got to first grade, I knew things about numbers that none of my classmates did. I knew the special significance of three special numbers: zero, one and infinity. The subtleties of these three numbers are not typically explored in depth until a student takes a college course in number theory. But, at six, I knew that zero is the first number in any measurement system and that it is the only number that, when added to another number, leaves the original number unchanged. I knew that the number one plays a similar role in multiplication. And, I knew that infinity is a number that is larger than any number you can count to.

Dad taught me how to read. The books he used to teach me were a lot tougher than the "Dick and Jane" books that were popular in schools at the time. I remember being a little tongue tied on some of the longer words. I also remember his patience when I was having a tough time. He was truly the best pal any boy could have.

We often talked about values. He stressed how wrong it is to lie, steal and cheat. He was a deeply religious man and he instilled strong moral values in me. Above all, he stressed the importance of truth and taught me that a scientist devotes his entire life to searching for and discovering truth.

At the end of our sessions, he would turn off the lamp. I would close my eyes and listen with fascination as he told me stories about men of science like Thomas Edison, Guglielmo Marconi and Albert Einstein. He also told me about aviation pioneers such as the Wright brothers, Charles Lindbergh and Howard Hughes. All were men of ability and boldness whose accomplishments had changed the world for the better. It was exciting to learn that the world had many heroes — many men like Dad. He filled me with confidence that, if I really worked hard, I could be just like these great men, that anything was possible for a hard-working, determined young man. I'm sure he was as happy as any father could be one evening when I said to him, "Dad, I know what I want to be when I grow up — I want to be a scientist."

Our Grier Avenue house's odd shape gave Dad an opportunity to add humor. It had a flat roof and looked like a pair of stacked cubes, the lower one slightly larger than the upper one. The second floor was set back from the lower and the flat front-porch roof was just outside of Dad's bedroom window. The bathroom was right next to the bedroom, and its window provided access to the porch roof.

Sometimes, Dad would get up and say he would be right back. In short order a disheveled man climbed through the bedroom window. He identified himself as Mr. Cratchet, a friend of Dad who lived in a piano box on the dump. Unlike Dad, he didn't wear glasses and his tie was halfway undone. I guess Dad thought that I was as easily fooled as Lois Lane. Cratchet insisted that his pal, Bob Wilcox, would be busy for a while and he wanted his friend from the piano box in the dump to keep me entertained. The charade — one he had also done with my brother many years earlier — was just fine with me. Mr. Cratchet had a fantastic sense of humor and made me laugh as he told his outrageous fibs.

CHAPTER 3. TRAGEDY

Visiting Dad's factory was another adventure that filled my days while I waited to start school. It was less than three-quarters of a mile from home, and I often made the walk alone. Even after the war ended, Dad employed mostly women. They all seemed cheerful and friendly, they must have really enjoyed their work. I loved being around them and all of Dad's machinery.

One of the biggest thrills of my life occurred when Dad convinced one of his good friends, a fellow named "Shoes" Lason, to take me for my first ride in an airplane. I really don't remember much about the flight. However, I'll never forget the excitement of the powerful forward thrust of the Piper Cub as it accelerated down the runway. The thrill of lifting off as we became airborne was incredible. The sensation I felt in my stomach was the most wonderful feeling I had ever experienced. The memory of that flight with "Shoes" Lason stayed with me long beyond my childhood. Years later as an adult, the first few times I flew, I always smiled as the airplane took off.

When I finally started school in 1950 I was definitely ready. From first to third grades I was a straight A student with a strong aptitude for mathematics. When my teachers asked if I had any idea what I wanted to do in life my answer was instantaneous — I was going to be a scientist. I received my first B in fourth grade but I continued being an A student in most of my classes.

Dad's business continued to prosper. We were the first family on our block to have a television set and, in 1953, Dad bought a brand new Kaiser. It was a car ahead of its time with a padded dashboard, a shatter-proof windshield and was very nicely styled compared to most of the dumpy looking cars of the era. Many automobiles would soon add the innovative features of Dad's Kaiser. He liked being different and owning a car made by Ford, General Motors or Chrysler was too ordinary for him.

Some of the kids in school teased me about Mom and Dad. Because both were in their fifties, they were old enough to be my grandparents. So, of course, my classmates were quick to point that fact out to me. While I was a little embarrassed about Mom I couldn't care less what they said about Dad. In effect, what I told them was, "You wish your Dad was as great as mine."

One of my school friends found out first hand how great Dad was. His mother was pregnant and she wanted a little extra income to help prepare for the baby. She asked me if I could speak to Dad about the possibility of her working for him. When I asked him, his answer made me smile with pride. "Of course son, just have her give me a ring."

─── • ───

Dad decided to manufacture model trolley cars that would run on standard O-gauge track. One of the factories close to Dad's on Brookside Drive specialized in plastic molding and manufactured the body and roof, which would be glued together. Dad manufactured the chassis and the electric motor. He designed an assembly line that would build the cars. Production began early enough to sell the trolley cars during the 1953 Christmas season.

It was an especially memorable Christmas for me. Mom and Dad gave me my first bicycle, which they had promised to do when I was ten. Technically, I was three weeks short of being ten. Thank heavens they weren't as rigid as the school board! The world suddenly became smaller. Now I could reach all points in Richardson Park within minutes. A bike did for a kid what an automobile did for his parents.

I had a couple of Dad's trolley cars scooting around the tracks of my Lionel train set. It was a really great toy. Unfortunately, the Lionel Train Company thought so too. There was a possibility that, before he had a chance to establish a market for his new

CHAPTER 3. TRAGEDY 39

product, Dad would face competition from a much larger company with a legendary name.

As far back as I can remember, Mom and Dad argued on a regular basis. Their bedroom was down the hallway from mine, and that's where they seemed to do most of their fighting. They quarreled with their door closed so I never could understand what they argued about. Their fighting intensified in 1953 and 1954.

During one especially long argument, my brother Bob closed my bedroom door in an attempt to shield me from the hostility. I stopped another one of their fights by simulating the way our dog, Josephine, sometimes wet on the floor. Poor Joe was now eighteen years old and had trouble controlling herself. When she had an accident in the house, she left a series of urine spots rather than a pool. I very carefully spit on the floor in a pattern that resembled one of Joe's accidents. "Mom," I called knocking on the bedroom door, "Joe just wet on my floor." It stopped the argument as she came to clean up the mess.

Dad was spending less time with me. About the only time I got to see him was at dinner and then he would go out again. This meant I spent a lot more time with Mom. Our relationship was quite different from the one I had with Dad. She scolded me, for example, when I received my first B. She constantly said to me, "why can't you be a good boy, like your brother Robert." Other times it was, "why can't you be a good boy, like Dicky." Dicky was my sister Betty's second child, Richard, who was a year younger than me. It seemed that I was always doing something that made Mom angry.

———•———

For me, the year 1954 was incredible. The biggest event was a vacation in California! Mom and I flew to Aunt Isabel's home in

Pleasant Hill, which is eighteen miles northeast of Oakland. The plan was that Dad and brother Bob would drive across country and join us. Then, we would drive south to the Los Angeles area and visit with Dad's younger brother, Stanley. We would conclude our vacation by driving home, stopping to see many of the beautiful places in the southwestern states.

The visit with Aunt Isabel added a second item to the list of things I wanted to do when I grew up. In addition to being a scientist, I wanted to move to California! Isabel's sons, Donald and Warren, were twelve and ten years older than me, respectively. I took an instant liking to Warren, who was like a big brother. Of course I had a big brother, Bob, but we hadn't spent much time together. He had gone away to college at the University of Delaware and now he was in the Air Force.

The days were hot in Pleasant Hill, but no matter how hot it had been, when the sun went down the temperature dropped to the point of being a bit chilly. Every evening, Warren and I would take sleeping bags out onto the back patio and sleep under the stars. We would talk, breathe the cool air and enjoy our view of the heavens. I was never cold, but it wasn't just the thick sleeping bag keeping me warm. I was basking in the warmth of my wonderful Aunt and my new buddy, Cousin Warren. I had found my own personal heaven on that patio in California.

After Dad and Bob arrived we visited Fisherman's Wharf in San Francisco and we took the boat cruise out to Alcatraz Prison in the Bay — I remember signs warning boats to avoid getting too close to the island. We then headed south toward Los Angeles to visit with Uncle Stanley, who lived in Whittier. The only thing I remember about our time in southern California was a trip we made to San Juan Capistrano Mission. It was wonderful having Dad around all the time — nothing else mattered.

CHAPTER 3. TRAGEDY

Figure 3.1: *Visiting Capistrano Mission in 1954. From left to right: Dad, me, Mom and Bob.*

The drive back home included a visit to Hoover Dam in Nevada. I remember looking down to the bottom of the massive dam and quickly stepping back. I experienced a sensation I had read about — I felt like I was being pulled over the side! We continued into Arizona and visited the Grand Canyon, Petrified Forest National Park and the Painted Desert. As many Americans of the era found, it was exciting traveling along the legendary Route 66.

I got a real kick out of reading the Burma Shave signs. They were a series of four or five small red signs with white letters spaced about a hundred feet apart on the roadside. You had to read each one to get the complete message. A typical series of five was "Are your whiskers — when you wake — tougher than — a two-bit steak? — Try Burma Shave." For me, our trip to California was a dream vacation.

Another wonderful thing happened in 1954 that reflected the times. With the exception of Fords, Mercurys and Lincolns, most 1954 automobiles had lines resembling those of World War II airplanes — the so-called "P-38 look." Automobile styling experienced dramatic changes as the 1955 models came to the marketplace in the fall. All three of the major U. S. auto makers introduced "jet-age" designs with pointed headlight frames, wraparound windshields, distinctive taillights and fenders with far less rounded shapes.

And the engines were much more powerful than they had been the year before. Horsepower increased from the 100-150 range to nearly 200 on most models. Even Chevrolet now had a V-8 engine for the first time. It was exciting beyond words for me as I marveled at magazines such as Popular Mechanics that displayed the new designs, including statistics on the powerful new engines. The age of the muscle car had begun — the average American would soon be driving a "hot rod."

There was a fire station on Maryland Avenue in Richardson Park, and very close to it was a Chevrolet dealer. I'll never forget the day I got my first closeup look at a brand-new 1955 Chevy. With its wide checkered grill, it looked like a large cat ready to leap into action. It was the most exciting automobile I had ever seen.

As a ten-year-old boy about to begin fifth grade, I was one happy young fellow. At this point in my life, it was hard to imagine things being any better. My dad was my best friend in the world and the world was changing in exciting ways. I felt optimistic and hopeful. I woke up every morning with a sense of excitement about what each new day would bring. And I was completely oblivious to the dark clouds that were gathering over my life and the violent storm they were bringing.

CHAPTER 3. TRAGEDY

——— • ———

Dad's investment in the model trolley cars had been a disaster. His quality control had been too lax. Many of his trolley cars were returned from merchants, often because the roofs came unglued. He lost his business and, even worse, he was forced to sell our home on Grier Avenue. Just one more payment had remained to pay off the mortgage on our home — Mom and Dad would have owned it outright. Now, instead of owning our home, we had to find a new place to live.

Dad found a new job as chief physicist for Pennsylvania based Hetherington, Inc. They provided him with a new shop in Richardson Park. He moved all of his coil-winding machines and other equipment to the new building. Although he no longer owned the business, he still worked independently.

Dad found a temporary home for us that was quite close to his new workplace, and it was quite a change from the home we had known. Bob was still in the Air Force stationed in Lake Charles, Louisiana, and he was very surprised when he came home for Christmas 1954. We were living in a trailer next to Dad's new shop!

Mom wasn't too happy about living in the trailer and decided to spend two months with Aunt Isabel. She and I returned to California and I attended school there. I enjoyed the stay, especially camping out on the patio every night with my pal Cousin Warren like we had done on the last visit. The highlight was Aunt Isabel teaching me to play the piano. She had me playing songs that were popular at the time such as "Ebb Tide," "Unchained Melody" and "I'll be Seeing You."

Returning to Delaware, we found an apartment in the small town of Hockessin, which is eight miles northwest of Wilmington, less than a mile from the Pennsylvania state line. I've always thought that, given his aversion to farm life, Dad made an odd choice since the apartment was right next to a farm. The worst part of living there was that we were very close to a building where they grew mushrooms. Judging by the smell of manure that was always evident in our apartment, we must have been directly downwind of that building. It was a huge relief when, in September 1955, we moved to an apartment in Clifton Park Manor on the northeast side of Wilmington.

There was a modernistic looking elementary school in the middle of Clifton Park Manor. It served the 900 families living in the Clifton Park community and many more in the Edgemoor neighborhood adjacent to the apartment complex. I began making new friends, mostly fellow sixth-graders.

Things had changed for the worse at home. As usual, Mom was always irritable and seemed to find fault in everything I did. But, I rarely ever saw Dad and it was bothering me a lot. My dismal home life increased my need for companionship from outside the confines of our apartment. Increasingly, I felt comfortable with my new neighborhood friends, many of whom were rebellious. It was easy to get caught up in their defiant and sometimes unruly adventures. The groundskeepers didn't like us riding our bikes on the grass, for example, and yelled at us every time we took a shortcut across the lawn. We sometimes responded by skidding our bikes through the flower beds in a semi-circular motion and pedaling away without ever leaving our bikes. It actually took some good timing and coordination to do it "properly."

Although I didn't see much of Dad, he did take me to his shop from time to time. He began teaching me how to use his drill press and his lathe. But, things had changed. He seemed more distant and troubled. His office was in the front of the shop and was completely enclosed, even at the top. There was room above

CHAPTER 3. TRAGEDY 45

his office to store things and, one afternoon, I climbed up to the top of his office to get something. When I did, I overheard him talking on the telephone. He seemed very happy, and I distinctly recall him saying, "I feel like a real pissaroo." I had no idea what this meant, but his elation was obvious.

I was confused. Dad had always been so happy to be around me, yet he seemed uneasy with me now. And who was he talking to on the phone that brought him so much joy? It sure wasn't Mom. I sensed that something wasn't right.

As the spring of 1956 came, my new buddies and I found a game that, like skidding through the flower beds, required good timing and coordination — hopping freight trains. We made our way to the train yards near the DuPont Edge Moor plant. We had to go down the hill, past the Merchandise Mart and across Governor Printz Boulevard to reach them. It was a short bike ride away. There was a depot nearby where the trains would stop to unload and reload. It was great sport running to catch a slow-moving train, ride along on the side of a freight car for a while and jump off when the train started gaining speed. We never did any damage to the trains and none of us was ever injured.

Nevertheless, railroad officials weren't too thrilled about what we were doing and decided to put a stop to it. I was one of several arrested for the crime of hopping freight trains. Actually, it was probably for trespassing. I had to go to Family Court and face a judge. I don't recall the penalty, but it was most likely either a warning or a small fine. Far more ominously, at twelve years of age, I was now considered to be a juvenile delinquent.

In mid May, Dad received the shocking news that his younger brother, Stanley, had died of a heart attack. He was only forty-nine. With both of his brothers gone — Stanley at forty-nine and Arthur at fifty-one — Dad was already older than both had lived to be. It is easy to understand how he would think that his days might be numbered. As he would explain in a letter to my sister Betty two months later, Dad was convinced that continuing to live with Mom would be "fatal to one or both of us."

——— • ———

On July 12, 1956, Mom and Dad were officially separated. Eight days later they were divorced. Mom was fifty-seven years old and her husband had divorced her after thirty-three years of marriage. He had left her with a twelve-year-old son who was showing increasing signs of rebelliousness that she didn't know how to deal with. She was very angry.

"Your father doesn't love you any more," she told me.

Dad had become very distant since we left Richardson Park. It was like being around a different person. Had he really stopped loving me? Was there something I did wrong? Had the embarrassment of being hauled into Family Court and being lectured by a judge convinced him that I was no good?

"He's run off with some damn hussy from the AA. He'd rather be with her than with you."

Is that who Dad had been talking to that day in the shop when I overheard his conversation on the phone? Was the man who had told me how wrong cheating is a hypocrite? Had he been cheating on Mom?

"He wouldn't know the truth if it kicked him in the teeth — he's been a damn liar all his life."

Even in our special times in his bedroom, Dad had pretended to be someone else. If he lied to me about being a bum who lived in a piano box on the dump, what else had he lied to me about?

"He was a damn drunk before you were born — you don't know the half of it — and so was that damn hussy he's taken up with — his wild-eyed get-rich-quick-schemes cost us everything we had — he spent every cent he made on God knows what — he pretends to be so pious, but he's just a damn cheat and a liar — you should be happy he's gone."

Mom's tirades against Dad went on for days. The things she said about him cut deep into my soul. I suppose she didn't realize the agony she was putting me through. I cried in bed every night. Everything I had trusted in and believed in had been washed away like a sand castle swept away by a wave. The great man I had loved and worshiped was gone. I wondered if he had never been a great man but just an illusion, a hollow shell of a person who didn't want me any more. So much had changed in just a little more than a year. As I awoke each morning I felt numb. The life I had known with my best friend in the world had been destroyed and the world seemed like a senseless, malevolent place. I was completely consumed by hopelessness and despair. I was starting to hate my dad.

In September we moved to Bellefonte, a community a mile northeast of Clifton Park. It was close to Mount Pleasant Junior High where I began seventh grade. School was boring. I was sick of arithmetic, yet school officials wouldn't place me in an advanced math class. Science was no better. I was developing much more interest in Major League Baseball, and my bubble-gum card collection was more important to me than doing my homework. It didn't really show up in my grades that much though because everything came so easily.

"I'm going to spend a month with Aunt Isabel," Mom said. "I can't afford the airfare for both of us, so you can stay with your father if you want." I agreed.

Soon after his divorce from Mom was final, Dad married Margaret Short who came from one of the Pennsylvania towns just north of Quakertown. She had belonged to the Elkton, Maryland

Alcoholics Anonymous and her aunt belonged to the Wilmington AA. Dad probably met her at an AA function. She was ten years younger than Dad — he was fifty-three and she was forty-three when they married. As I recall, my step Mom "Peggy" was an attractive woman who wanted very much to be close with me.

They lived in Newport, a small town just over a mile southwest of our old house in Richardson Park. It was a nice house in a relatively new housing development. It was a peaceful setting both outdoors and indoors; there was no arguing between Dad and his new wife. Both were warm and kind to me, but they must have been disappointed by my cynical indifference toward them. I didn't talk with them very much. Rather, I spent most of my time in my bedroom playing rock-and-roll records and talking to my Clifton Park friends on the telephone.

Dad tried to explain why he and Mom had divorced. His words revealed no bitterness and he said nothing negative about Mom. The only thing I remember him saying about her was, "David, your mother changed." He seemed to be very happy with Peggy, and the absence of constant bickering and arguing spoke for itself.

But my heart was so hardened against him because of what I considered his betrayal of me that nothing he said made any difference. As the date of Mom's return from California approached, I decided that I would strike back at him for the way he had hurt me. Without saying goodbye, I left a day early and pedaled my bike back to Bellefonte. The apartment manager unlocked the door so I could get into the apartment and await Mom's return.

A day or two later I spoke with Dad on the telephone. The thing I remember most about the conversation was that he said, "I wish you could have at least said goodbye to Peggy — she was very hurt." He didn't mention how it made him feel.

Chapter 4

Destruction

Who so neglects learning in his youth, loses the past and is dead for the future. – Euripides

Our Bellefonte apartment was the second story of an elderly couple's home. A huge tree had shed its leaves, covering the lawn with an autumn blanket of red, yellow and brown hues — far more colorful than my gray mood. I had awakened feeling angry for a reason I couldn't quite identify. When our landlord asked me to rake the leaves I obliged, hoping that the fresh air might help. The slightly pungent fragrance of the freshly fallen leaves lifted my spirits and so did the distant sound of drums as the band performed at the nearby Mount Pleasant High School football game.

On his way to the game, one of my new friends who lived a couple blocks away, Billy, rode up on his English bike. His was the fastest bike in the neighborhood and he really knew how to ride. Nobody could beat him in a bike race. Most guys had American bikes with a single sprocket. Billy's bike had three or four speeds and he knew how to shift gears with perfection. He noticed the bent spokes on my bike by the side of the house.

"What happened to your back wheel?" he asked.

"Oh, some guy kicked it yesterday," I replied, "I had a pretty tough time making it up the hill from Clifton Park last night, but I can still ride it. I just need to straighten the spokes." I didn't see any point in telling him about breaking the Clifton Park apartment managers' window.

"What you need is a new bike — those American models with big, fat tires are too slow."

"You have a father, I don't!" I screamed at my friend.

I was as startled as he was at the vehemence of my reaction to his advice. It was the first time I had acknowledged that I no longer had a father in my home — that I had been abandoned — that I was angry about my miserable state. For months I had said very little about it. I had been almost completely silent. All of my pent up emotions finally burst out of me in uncontrollable rage. Regaining my composure I added, "I can't afford a new bike."

"Sorry man, I didn't mean anything by it. See ya' — I'm goin' to the football game," Billy replied as he pedaled away.

It really didn't matter anyway. Mom and I would be leaving for Lake Charles, Louisiana right after the end of the year and my bike wouldn't be coming with us. There was certainly no point in buying a new one. We were going to live with my brother Bob, who was still in the Air Force training as a navigator-bombardier on a Boeing B-47 Stratojet, the world's first swept-wing bomber.

"Will we ever stop moving?" I thought. "Every time I make new friends we move to a new place. Now it's all the way to Louisiana and another school. Mom said they're still fighting the Civil War down there. I don't wanna go."

———•———

Lake Charles sits on the banks of the Calcasieu River in the southwestern part of Louisiana, approximately thirty miles from

CHAPTER 4. DESTRUCTION

the Texas state line. First settled in 1852, its growth began after the Homestead Act of 1862, which brought a first wave of settlers. Even more settlers came after the Civil War ended. Its timber industry developed rapidly in the latter part of the nineteenth century and farms proliferated, with rice becoming the area's foremost commercial crop. The development of railroads accelerated the area's population growth and local industry continued to expand. After World War II, Lake Charles developed a petrochemical refining industry, which added to the city's prosperity.

One of Lake Charles' most famous residents in 1957 was St. Louis Cardinals shortstop Alvin Dark. I recall seeing a big sign with his picture at a baseball field that got my attention because I was intrigued by Major League Baseball and its plethora of statistics. Dark was near the end of an excellent career in the majors, and would go on to manage for many years after his playing days ended. His trade to the Cardinals by the Giants during the 1956 season made Lake Charles baseball fans happy since they rooted for St. Louis, the closest Major League team. They would be thrilled that, playing alongside the great Stan Musial, hometown hero Dark would hit .290 in the 1957 season and help lead the Cardinals to a strong second-place finish.

Dark was a rookie with the Boston Braves in 1946 when the U. S. Army deactivated "Lake Charles Army Air Field." Originally a local airport, the U. S. Army took over its operation for use as an Army base during World War II to train crews for B-26 bombers. With the onset of the Cold War, the base reopened in the Spring of 1951 under the name "Lake Charles Air Force Base." It was part of America's Strategic Air Command, which was the Air Force's global bomber fleet. Like any Air Force Base, it added to the city's prosperity with all of the Air Force personnel, their dependents and their purchasing power.

Figure 4.1: *My brother Bob was trained by the Air Force as a navigator-bombardier for the Boeing B-47 Stratojet, which was the world's first swept-wing bomber.*

As I quickly learned, like in any town with a military base, many Lake Charles residents resented Air Force personnel and their dependents. The resentment was especially pronounced toward "yankees" — people who came from the hated Union states.

I attended Rosteet Junior High and inadvertently brought unwanted attention to myself. I had never been exposed to people who speak with a heavy southern drawl, such as my history teacher. As fate would have it, we were studying the Civil War. When we got to General Sherman's advance across the state of Georgia, I could not understand what she was talking about when she said, "Sherman *rurnt* Georgia."

"What did Sherman do to Georgia?" I asked.

"He *rurnt* Georgia," she repeated.

"I don't understand what *rurnt* means — can you spell it for me," I requested in complete innocence and sincerity.

"It's R-U-I-N-E-D," she obliged.

This exchange apparently didn't set well with my Louisiana classmates. With hindsight, I'm sure they must have thought I was making fun of her. I wasn't.

CHAPTER 4. DESTRUCTION

At lunch time a few of the boys asked me where I was born. I explained that I was born in Wilmington, Delaware and that I had come to live with my brother who was stationed at the Air Force base. Because Bob had warned me about local resentment toward military dependents, I knew that being an Air Force "brat" was strike one. They told me that they knew part of Delaware had sided with the south and part with the north during the Civil War. And then came the all-important question.

"Is Wilmington north or south of the Mason-Dixon line?"

I knew the answer, and I knew that if I answered correctly it was certainly strike two. "Gee, I don't know," I lied.

Given what unfolded the next day, one or more of those boys had obviously checked with somebody who knew about geography. They told me that Wilmington was north of the Mason-Dixon line and that made me a "yankee." I didn't see much point in noting that the line actually ended at the Maryland-Delaware border, since that would have shown that I had known more than what I told them the day before. I knew I was in deep stuff!

During a recess, I was sitting alone in a corner of the playground. Soon, several of my classmates formed a circle around me. A few threw their pencils at me. They were taunting me and I was suddenly about as scared as I had ever been in my life. I was about to have the living daylights beat out of me, all because I was a "yankee" and my brother was in the Air Force — things over which I had no control. As their taunting approached a fever pitch, an incredible thing happened. A dark-haired boy pushed through the circle and came up next to me.

"Anybody goin' mess wi' him, goin' mess wi' me."

Those were the most courageous words I had ever heard spoken — and I didn't even know the person who said them! The circle of angry boys dispersed and soon just the two of us remained.

I looked at him in astonishment and puzzlement. He answered my unstated question.

"I'm Frank Smith. My Dad's an Air Force cook. I figur' us Air Force guys gotta stick together."

I soon learned that Frank was the toughest guy in the school and nobody *ever* messed with him. Hailing from Picayune, Mississippi, Frank had a strong moral foundation and was nothing like the rowdy crowd I had been hanging around with back home. He loved Elvis Presley and I thought Elvis was great, too — that became a common bond between us. For the rest of the time I spent in Lake Charles, Frank was my closest friend.

I really didn't need a bike to get around, especially since Frank's house was close to mine and that's where I spent a lot of time. When we needed to travel around the city we took the bus. Buses ran all over the city and got us where we wanted to go pretty quickly.

It was on those buses that I had my first close up view of segregation and racial discrimination. The buses in Lake Charles had signs near the back that read "colored." Only white people were allowed to sit near the front. I found those "colored" signs to be very disturbing and I felt sad for the few blacks I saw obediently seated in the back. I remember thinking what it would be like if that sign read "Air Force dependents" or "yankees." It would have made me mad as hell, and I remember thinking that I would have been inclined to throw a large rock through the window of the bus company's headquarters.

One of the more exciting things I did in Lake Charles also involved transportation. Bob had a motor scooter and he taught me how to ride it. Of course, he made sure I didn't venture beyond the street we lived on because I was too young to operate it around the city. The clutch was on one side of the handle

CHAPTER 4. DESTRUCTION 55

bars. You shifted gears on the other side. The most difficult part to master was smoothly engaging the clutch in low gear to get the motor scooter moving. Shifting gears was very easy by comparison, and it didn't take me long to master operation of the scooter. It was a skill I would make use of when we returned to Wilmington — in ways Bob had certainly not intended!

In April 1957, after I had spent a little more than three months in Louisiana, Bob was discharged from the Air Force. After the turbulent start with my history-class misunderstanding and Frank Smith's heroic schoolyard rescue of me, the visit had been uneventful. I stayed out of trouble the entire time, largely because Frank was such a positive influence.

——— • ———

My return to Delaware landed me in my fourth different school for seventh grade, namely, P. S. du Pont High in north Wilmington, about two miles southwest of Mt. Pleasant High. Bob and Mom rented a house two blocks from the school. I'm sure the plan was to keep me away from my rowdy friends from Clifton Park and Mt. Pleasant. I didn't need a bike and, at thirteen, I no longer had any interest in pedaling around on one. I was a teenager after all — riding a bike was for little kids.

School continued to be boring. However, my grades were beginning to reflect my lack of interest in learning. While I would earn an A in math and science classes, English and social studies were a different matter. I was having difficulty maintaining even a C in those classes.

It didn't take long to make new friends. At first, I hooked up with boys who were as intrigued by baseball as I was. I studied the batting and pitching statistics that were published every Sunday in the newspaper, and I could recite the starting lineups for all sixteen Major League teams. Since the Philadelphia Phillies were the closest team to Wilmington, I rooted for them. Their pitching superstar Robin Roberts was a legend who made the Phillies one of the best teams in the pros on the days that he pitched. But, the Phillies were on the decline in 1957. The team was aging and showed no signs of regaining the excellence that had taken them to the 1950 World Series. Roberts had lost a little zip on his fastball and he had a tough 1956 season, failing to win twenty games for the first time since 1949. He would lose twenty-two during the summer of 1957.

The only thing I recall about the summer of 1957 was Bob taking me to a Phillies game — they were playing the Cincinnati Reds. What I remember most was a late-inning confrontation between a Phillies relief pitcher and Reds slugger Ted Kluszewski, who rarely ever struck out but was hampered by a back injury. After he fouled off several pitches, referring to the Phillies' pitcher, Bob said, "If he strikes Kluszewski out, this crowd will give him a standing ovation." Battling through his pain, Kluszewski denied the crowd its opportunity for that ovation. He hit a couple more fouls, finally found a pitch he liked and bounced the ball off the outfield fence for a double.

When school started again in September of 1957, I was an eighth grader. It was another boring year of arithmetic and virtually nothing to hold my interest. I was making more new friends who, with hindsight, were far worse than the Mt. Pleasant crowd Bob and Mom wanted to get me away from. Because I disliked English and social studies classes, I discovered that it was more enjoyable to skip the classes and hang around the corner store a block from the high school with an older group of boys. And when I wasn't hanging around the store, I was often sitting with them in detention at the principal's office for being disruptive in class or for being caught hanging around the store. Many

CHAPTER 4. DESTRUCTION 57

of my new friends were sixteen and had their own cars, which made them very popular. Having friends with cars also solved the transportation problem. Bikes were permanently out — cars were in.

One of my new-found friends discovered that Chevrolets of that era had an unusual feature. The key switch on the dashboard looked like a duck's bill. You had to turn the switch as far as it would go counterclockwise before extracting the key to lock it. If the driver left the switch in the vertical position, all you had to do was grip the switch between thumb and forefinger and turn it clockwise to start the car — no key required!

Inevitably, we decided to take advantage of this design misfeature of Chevys. We waited until it was dark and checked the Chevys parked on the street. When we found one with an unlocked ignition switch, our fun began. We piled into the car and took it for a ride. Most of the Chevys we took our joy rides in had a standard transmission, so you could only drive if you could handle a clutch and a gear-shift lever. When it was my turn to drive, I discovered that it was not much of a transition from using my hands on a motor scooter to using my feet in a car. I very quickly mastered driving a "stick shift."

Although it inconvenienced the cars' owners, we rationalized, we weren't damaging their cars. We weren't being malicious, we were just having fun. We saw it as no more than a prank, never thinking about the danger to ourselves and to others. The thought of someone needing his car for a medical emergency never entered our minds. But, none of us cared about anyone but ourselves — we had taken charge of our lives and we did as we pleased.

This went on for weeks and we probably took joyrides in a dozen or more cars. We were never caught in the act. Yet, toward the end of 1957, the police arrested me and a couple of my friends. They knew we had been "stealing" cars and checking our fingerprints proved it. We would all be going to reform school.

I would later learn that one of the older boys — a fellow I considered to be one of my best friends — told the police who was taking all of the joyrides in neighborhood Chevys. He had been arrested for several more-serious crimes and had traded what he knew about us in exchange for the police dropping some of the charges against him.

Dad was shocked at how badly things were going for me. In early January 1958 he arranged to pick me up so he could find out first hand what I was thinking and to offer me an alternative to reform school. He drove me to Richardson Park near where he used to have his Wilmington Coil Company factory on Brookside Drive. He surprised me when he pulled his car to the side of the street and told me to take the wheel. "Drive down to the end of the block, turn around and bring the car back to where we are now," he commanded. When I completed the short drive, his first words to me were, "David, you aren't a very good driver."

I'm sure he went on to discuss how dangerous it was for me to be driving, but nothing he said left as strong an impression on me as his assessment of my driving skills. All I could think of was that he was disappointed in me — and for much more than my shaky driving ability. I felt very bad about that.

He told me he had worked out a plan that would save me from reform school. With the help of his lawyer friend, Hiram Warder, and the pastor of his church, Reverend Charles Priebe, he had arranged for me to go to *Boy's Town* in Nebraska. He had spoken with the juvenile authorities and they had agreed to let me go there rather than to Ferris School for Boys.

As a grown man, I can look back and understand just how desperately Dad wanted to help me. He must have done a lot of

CHAPTER 4. DESTRUCTION

pleading and persuading to make the *Boy's Town* option possible. But, as a fourteen-year-old boy who was angry with him, I had a completely different perspective.

When he showed me a brochure about *Boy's Town*, all I could think of was, "Here we go again — I'll have to move and find new friends." He wanted me to think about it before making my decision. There was nothing to think about, so I told him straight out, "No Dad, I don't want to go there. And I don't want to talk about it anymore."

─── • ───

The engine purred as the driver accelerated. He shifted to second gear and released the clutch with the smoothness of a tag-team roller skater, like the ones I had seen at the roller rink. The engine was both quiet and obviously powerful as he continued accelerating. "They must've just tuned it up," I thought. He shifted into high gear just as smoothly. "Too bad the muffler's so quiet — it would really sound cool with a Hollywood muffler." A couple of the guys from P. S. du Pont High had Hollywood mufflers, and their deep-pitched sound made a car sound very powerful.

There were six of us headed to Ferris School for Boys in the police van. The back of the van had benches on each side. The driver was in the cab, which was separated from the back compartment. There was a small window that gave a view of the driver's police cap and part of the windshield. Another policeman was in the compartment with us, seated just at the cab end between the benches. Three of us were white kids and the other three were black. All of us were either fourteen or fifteen except for one of the black boys — he was sixteen. He would go to Dunbar Cottage with the older black kids at Ferris. The other two blacks would go to Grace Cottage and the rest of us to Ball Cottage.

It was February 26, 1958 and I had just been sentenced to Ferris, which was Delaware's reform school. I would be there for at least six months and, if I behaved badly, for as long as a year. Although I didn't realize it at the time, the day before had been Dad's birthday and the next day would be Mom's. Both must have viewed this day as their worst birthday present ever. But, I wasn't thinking of them. To me it was an inconvenience that I could deal with, especially since several of my pals from both the Clifton Park and Wilmington neighborhoods were either already there or would be in another week or so.

Life at Ferris School was very regimented. It might not have been so bad if the large, one-armed man in charge hadn't been so strict and ill tempered. He and his wife ran Ball Cottage with iron fists and no apparent concern whatever for the boys in their charge. I suppose they felt they had to be strict to maintain control, but their callous demeanor earned them the hatred of just about every boy in the cottage. From time to time they would have a weekend off and a far warmer man would run the cottage without losing control of the boys. The contrast served to intensify my hatred of the one-armed man and his wife.

There were no fences around Ferris School, which made it more like an extremely rigid boarding school than a jail. Nevertheless, there were constant reminders of where we were. Every morning boys from all four cottages would line up and they would count us to make sure no one had run away. While the black boys were segregated from the white boys with regard to living quarters, we did share things like the gymnasium. I made friends with several black boys, and it would serve me well in the years to come in unexpected ways.

Ferris had a school that went up to eighth grade. One of my teachers had a long Polish name and decided to go by Mr. K so

CHAPTER 4. DESTRUCTION

people wouldn't have difficulty addressing him. He taught the science class, and he usually made it mildly interesting. Based on my outstanding test scores I was clearly one of his best students. It seemed obvious that I was going to earn an A in his class.

But then, something happened that changed his view of me. In class one day he told us that, "When a sponge has absorbed as much water as it possibly can, we call it the point of no return"

"That's not right Mr. K," I said, "it's the saturation point."

"No it isn't!" he snapped, startling the entire class.

"Well, I'm certain it's the saturation point," I told him, "maybe you should check your science book."

Mr. K was furious with me for contradicting him. He did a poll of the other boys in the class, which found them agreeing with him. Having witnessed his display of anger toward me, I'm sure that none of my classmates dared to be at odds with him. When the school year ended, I received a B in science, despite having one of the highest overall test-score averages in the class.

As springtime came we spent more time outside. There was a softball field just outside the cottage and every day we would choose teams. I quickly showed that I could hit a softball farther than most of the other boys. I wasn't a very good fielder, but that made no difference. I just played the outfield where I wouldn't have to handle the ball very often. I was always one of the first people chosen when teams were selected.

I decided to keep my batting statistics, and every night after a game I would update them. I was very strict in my score keeping on myself and never included getting on base on an error as a hit. By the end of the summer of 1958, I hit 66 home runs and had a batting average over .400.

Ferris School officials assembled a hardball team consisting of the best players in Ball and Grace Cottages. Based on my batting prowess and constant hustle, I made the team's starting lineup. We did reasonably well in the games we played with what were probably Junior High School teams. I made even more black friends on our hardball team.

In one game, we were being clobbered by a particularly arrogant team. They were ahead by eight or nine runs and they were heckling us. It really made me angry and I started telling everybody in the dugout to try harder — to show these big mouths that we weren't quitters. My black friends joined in, yelling encouragement to every batter. Suddenly, we had the bases loaded and I was the batter. The pitcher quickly got two strikes on me. One of his teammates told him to let me hit it. And hit it I did — he served up a pitch that I ripped into left field. It was a wicked line drive that sailed just over the outfielder's glove and rolled all the way to the highway at the end of the field. I crossed home plate before they got the ball back to the infield. My grand-slam home run changed a blowout into a real contest — we turned the tables and taunted them. While a few more of my teammates crossed home plate before the game ended, we came up a couple runs short. It didn't matter though. We had salvaged our pride and we all snickered when we heard their coach screaming at them as their bus headed toward the highway.

Although I didn't realize it at the time, I had just shown how much difference positive leadership can make — leadership I had provided. While I didn't appreciate the full meaning of what I had done, my fellow teammates certainly benefitted. And it cemented my relationship with the black boys from Grace Cottage.

Mom came to visit me on every visiting day. She never let me down and it was a relief from the drudgery and regimentation of life in reform school. Because Ferris had a family-occasion policy, I was able to go to my brother Bob's wedding in June. I

CHAPTER 4. DESTRUCTION

recall that Bob's bride, Maureen, was stunning, especially with her big, beautiful eyes. Mom told me she would be living with them in Kynlyn Apartments, a few blocks from our old apartment in Bellefonte. I was disappointed that Dad wasn't at the wedding. Bob was still angry with him and had refused to invite Dad's new wife. It was just as well because Mom had threatened to "scratch her eyes out" if she had come. Dad sent a nice present and politely declined the invitation.

Dad didn't decline the opportunity to spend time with me. Because of the divorce, Ferris authorities agreed to let him have special visiting days. He would come on Sundays and we would sit in his car and talk. And we quickly found a great deal to talk about thanks to the summer course I was taking at Bayard School in Wilmington. It was a course in physics with a strong focus on electricity — Dad's specialty! I was excited by what I was learning in the course and I wanted to share my excitement with someone. Although things were a little strained at first, Dad quickly won me over. He was calm and he was patient. Unlike Mom, he didn't lecture me about how I had to stop being so disobedient and wild. He was far more interested in discussing math and physics. I can remember a few snippets of our conversations in his car.

"I'll be starting algebra in September, Dad — what's algebra like?"

"It's real mathematics. Arithmetic is something you had to learn to prepare for algebra. I'm sure you'll find it to be a lot more interesting."

I told him about the B that Mr. K had given me in the Ferris science class. His response was one of the most profound things he ever said to me. Although I can't remember Dad's precise words, in effect, what he said to me was, "David, I'm more proud of you that you stood your ground and received a B. You were right and he was wrong. I taught a similar course during World War II and, if a student had questioned me, I would have checked my sources. If I had been wrong I would have told the whole class. Science is all about truth, son. Your teacher is certainly no scientist if he acts like that."

During another visit, I told Dad about an idea I had for a perpetual-motion machine — a machine that runs forever without power. It wasn't a very good idea, and he explained to me how even the tiniest amount of friction would stop such a machine. He also pointed out that even if it worked, it would be no more than a toy — you wouldn't be able to get it to do anything useful. Then he told me about a perpetual-motion motor he had devised as a young man. He asked if I knew how an electric motor worked. When I correctly explained how a single-armature electric motor works, he smiled. Then, he told me what his idea was. It was very simple and truly ingenious. All he needed was a material that would block a magnetic field. Unfortunately, he explained, all materials either let a magnetic field pass through them or they become magnetized. Either way, it made his motor design impossible.

On September 28, 1958, Dad made his usual Sunday visit. We had a wonderful time. I had started ninth grade, and the Ferris officials approved my attending Mt. Pleasant Junior High. I was finally learning algebra, and I was elated because of it. Dad was right, this was real mathematics. I told him how happy I was that my math and science classes were challenging and enjoyable, and that I was especially pleased to have excellent teachers for both. But, far more important, Dad was back. He was the same wonderful man I had known as a young boy. When he left, I had already begun to anticipate his next visit.

CHAPTER 4. DESTRUCTION

•

The next day I received the news that Dad would not be coming to visit me ever again. He had died of a massive heart attack a few hours after his visit with me.

I was permitted to go home and stay with Mom, Bob and Maureen until after Dad's funeral. I was stunned when Mom said she would not attend the funeral. "Did she hate him that much?" I thought. I had to know how she really felt about Dad now that he was truly gone.

"Do you still love him?" I asked. She didn't respond. I asked again, refusing to let her silence stand. Still no answer. "Answer me!" I demanded. She finally relented, and in a near whisper said, "Yes."

Bob, Maureen and I went to Dad's viewing. As I approached his lifeless body, I was overtaken by the most intense pain I had ever experienced. The man I had loved so much as a young boy, who had gone away for a while and had finally returned to love me again was lying in his casket. I couldn't understand why life had been so cruel to tear him away from me again — I fully understood the permanence of his death. I threw myself to the floor in front of his casket, screaming and pounding my fists on the floor. My niece, Carole, tried to come to me but her father held her back. She would tell me many years later that, "It left a lasting impression of despair and hopelessness, something I might have read into it but can still feel today when I think about it."

My brother Bob took me out of the room and we both sat and cried together. Bob was feeling remorse partly because in siding with Mom he had, in effect, excluded Dad from his wedding, and now his wife Maureen had met her father in law for the first time as he lay in the funeral home. Bob and I would discover many years later that we were both experiencing the same emotion.

Neither of us would ever have a chance to reconcile things with Dad. Neither of us would ever be able to say we were sorry for being so cold toward him after he divorced Mom. Neither of us would ever be able to tell him how much we loved him.

———•———

I kept to myself after Dad's funeral. Life seemed so pointless with all of its disappointments. Every time I found something to be happy about it would be snatched away. I had heard people all my life telling me to be careful to avoid getting my hopes up too high in order to avoid being let down when things didn't turn out the way I hoped they would. The cynics and the spirit crushers were winning the battle for my soul.

My only joy in life was algebra. It was incredible how much I enjoyed it and how easily it came to me. I enjoyed the challenge of solving each new problem and took great delight at meeting the challenge head on and succeeding almost without effort. I loved the purity and strict adherence to logic that mathematics embodies. I asked if I could be moved into the advanced math class, but Mt. Pleasant officials thought I should not try to "bite off more than I could chew."

As I reflect back on these times, I realize that the advice I was receiving about lowering expectations ran counter to what Dad had taught me. His vision of the world was far more healthy for a young person who begins life with hopes and dreams of an exciting future. While people who advise young people against biting off more than they can chew may mean well, they encourage mediocrity and timidity at the expense of creativity and self confidence.

In January 1959 I was released from Ferris and went home to Mom's new apartment in Clifton Park Manor. Thankfully, I would make it through ninth grade without changing schools. It was the first time that had happened since sixth grade.

Mom had a six-month lease on the apartment and we had to decide where to live after June. I persuaded her to move back to Wilmington and she agreed. I had more friends in that neighborhood and that made it my first preference. She found a house within walking distance of P. S. du Pont High.

Reading the newspapers I discovered that something incredible had happened during the 1958 baseball season. The Pittsburgh Pirates, who had been one of the worst teams in the majors for a decade, had jumped from last place in 1957 to a surprising second-place finish behind the Milwaukee Braves. With budding new stars like Roberto Clemente, Bill Mazeroski, Dick Stuart and a maturing pitching staff, the team held promise for greatness in the future. The Phillies had hit rock bottom, finishing last in 1958. It was time for a team change.

I read that the Pirates had a great announcer named Bob Prince, and that he could be heard on radio station KDKA. I remembered Dad telling me that this was a very powerful radio station in Pittsburgh and that it had been one of the very first. One evening I carefully tuned my radio and, although there was some static, I found the Pirate broadcast. Bob Prince was as good as advertised. The matter was settled — I was a Pirate fan!

Thanks to an incredible year by relief pitcher Elroy Face who compiled a won-lost record of 18-1, the Pirates won all but two of their extra inning games during the 1959 season. I was tuned in to KDKA and heard one of the losses. The Pirate pitcher was Harvey Haddix and he was facing the Milwaukee Braves who had won the pennant in 1957 and 1958. He pitched a perfect game for twelve innings, but the Pirates failed to score. I agonized when an error ended the perfect game in the bottom of the thirteenth inning and the Braves went on to score. Poor Harvey Haddix lost the best game he ever pitched!

At this point in my life I decided that college was probably not in my future. There was no money to pay for school, according to Mom, and my grades were good only in math and science. Anything that required memorization, such as history, gave me a great deal of difficulty. It didn't help any that I found such classes to be uninspiring and uninteresting. So, I opted for the business curriculum at P. S. du Pont rather than the college-preparatory option. I would be taking courses like mechanical drawing and typing.

In math class I was studying plane geometry. I found it to be interesting, but far less exciting than algebra had been. Geometry is much more of an exercise in logic as opposed to practical problem solving in algebra. I found myself impatient with having to remember all of the axioms and hypotheses that are essential to learning the subject.

I was the only boy in the typing class and that was great. I always had a girlfriend from third or fourth grade on and now I had an opportunity to pick from a large group of good-looking girls. However, before I could cash in on this opportunity, I made a decision that changed everything.

January 1960 was approaching, and I would soon be sixteen. That meant I would be able to get a license to drive. I had a $75 savings bond that Mom and Dad bought me during World War II and it had just matured. That was enough money to buy a car such as a '51 Ford. Since I would need money for gas and insurance, I would have to find a job. To make all of this "easier," in November 1959, I decided to quit school. After all, I figured, the main thing that had held my interest in school was math, and I really wasn't enjoying geometry.

CHAPTER 4. DESTRUCTION

Disaster struck in December. A friend from the Clifton Park area stole a car and drove it to my neighborhood. He picked me up at a corner drugstore where my friends and I hung out every night. I knew the car was stolen, but I suppose I saw it as an opportunity to practice driving in preparation for the driving test I would have to take to get my license in January. Bad decision! We were pulled over and arrested. My friend assured the police that I had nothing to do with taking the car. It didn't matter though because we had both spent time in reform school. We had to serve a one-year probation period after being released from Ferris, which included a prohibition on associating with other boys who had spent time in Ferris. Because of this probation violation, I was returned to Ferris to serve the balance of my probation period.

Even though I would be there for a little less than two months, I couldn't bear the idea of being under the thumb of that hateful one-armed man in Ball Cottage. Within two days I ran away from Ferris. I trudged across the ice and snow and tried to make my way home, but the police soon caught up with me. They held me in the city jail overnight so I could face a Family-Court judge the next morning. When I told the judge I refused to stay at Ferris, he told me he would have to put me in a place where I would stay. "I hereby remand you to the First Offenders Building at the New Castle County Correctional Institution."

The New Castle County Correctional Institution was more commonly referred to as the "Workhouse" — it was a polite way of referring to the state prison. The First Offenders Building was a separate building for younger offenders located within the prison fences that had barbed wire at the top. There were guard towers at every corner of the prison, two within view of the First Offenders Building. The guards had rifles and would shoot anyone who might try to escape or be part of a prison disturbance.

I was just fifteen years old and now I had a prison record. "What a lousy break," I thought. In my view, I hadn't done anything to deserve it.

I found the First Offenders Building easier to take than Ferris. Some of my reform-school buddies had also found their way to prison, so I wasn't lonesome. There were many boys in their late teens and a few young adults serving sentences as long as seven years for offenses like armed robbery. There were also a couple of men doing life sentences for murder. The prison officials had found the lifers' behavior in prison to be exemplary and sent them to the First Offenders Building rather than confining them to the main part of the prison, which was called the "big house."

I was relieved that the guards were not as hateful as the one-armed man at Ferris. Some actually joked with us and, as long as we stayed in line, they weren't too hard on us. Because of bad behavior the year before at Ferris, I hadn't been permitted to spend the 1958 holidays with my family. So, for the second year in a row, I would spend Christmas behind bars.

The First Offenders Building had a small library where I found a first-year algebra book with lots of homework problems and answers listed in the back. I passed my time by solving the problems and checking with the answers section to confirm that my solutions were correct. By the time I was released in January 1960, I had worked every problem in the book.

Soon after I "hit the streets," I applied for and obtained my driver's license. Cashing in my savings bond and persuading Mom to add $25, I bought a black 1951 Ford for $100. It wasn't much of a car, but it made me happy. It made Mom happy too because I drove her anywhere she needed to go. She didn't drive because of a bad experience when Dad tried to teach her — she ran into a large rock and decided to leave the driving to others.

CHAPTER 4. DESTRUCTION

I had no luck finding work and I began to realize that quitting school had been a bad idea. With hindsight, I'm sure spending time with that algebra book in the Workhouse reignited my interest in math and learning. Also, Mom's pleading with me to give tenth grade another try helped. To top it all off, a couple of my friends even encouraged me to get back into school.

When I finally decided that going back to school was the best thing I could do, I opted to attend Mt. Pleasant. It was a much better school than P. S. du Pont from an academic point of view. The teachers were better and I had learned a lot more when I was there. In June of 1960 Mom and I moved back to Clifton Park Manor for the third time.

Because my '51 Ford was falling apart, it was becoming clear that I needed a new car. Mom had a pretty good job in the Merchandise Mart and decided to help me out, so long as I promised to drive her to and from work. I agreed and started looking for a new car. In mid July I found a 1952 Ford for $150. Within a week, I tore up the transmission's first gear in a drag race. I would have to find the money to fix it, which was a big problem because I had no job and Mom couldn't afford to fix it.

Like so many young people who find themselves in and out of trouble for relatively minor offenses, I decided to raise the stakes. Late one night after drinking with my Wilmington friends, I decided to drive alone to the south side of Wilmington near the junkyards. There were several gas stations along the main highway, all of which closed at midnight. I broke a window and entered one of the stations. I found the cash box and it contained just a couple dollars. I returned to my car, drove to another station, broke its window and found a few coins. I repeated this in two or three more gas stations. My total haul was less than twenty dollars — certainly not enough to fix my transmission.

As I got back in my car to leave the last gas station a police car pulled up. I sped away and the police car followed. He chased me all the way to the Maryland state line, where he ended his pursuit. I kept driving until I came to Havre de Grace, Maryland, which is thirty miles southwest of Wilmington. I slept in my car that night.

The next morning I drove back to the Delaware state line and removed the license plate. I assumed the cop chasing me had written down the plate number and I would be nailed if the police caught sight of me. I would have to gamble that I wouldn't be pulled over for driving a car without a license plate. I drove to a junkyard and called a friend to pick me up. I was going to abandon the car and figure out a way to leave the state for good. Before my friend arrived, I checked my car to see if I had forgotten anything. The detective who had chased me pulled up next to my car. I'll never know if someone tipped him off or if he was just doing a routine patrol. Either way, I was under arrest for fourth-degree burglary, which was a felony.

My offenses meant another trip to the Wilmington courthouse, an attractive structure adjacent to symbols of Delaware's heritage. Directly across the street lies Rodney Square, which includes a statue of Revolutionary War hero Caesar Rodney. On the other side of Rodney Square lies the duPont Building, another name inextricably linked to Delaware. I wasn't fearful when I appeared before a judge in September. Instead, I felt an irrational sense of pride that the state of Delaware had decided to try me as an adult. Although I know it wasn't what they intended, it made me feel that the state recognized me as having grown up faster than most boys. Because my crimes were about as minor a felony that Delaware had on its books, the judge sentenced me to three years probation. With hindsight, it's clear that I had dodged a bullet.

CHAPTER 4. DESTRUCTION

Getting off so lightly left the dark side of me with an odd sense of arrogance. Although I hadn't gotten away with much to speak of, I had nevertheless gotten away with what I had done. I saw life as being pointless and the universe I was living in as being cold and without comfort. So, getting little more than a slap on the hand for the worst thing I had ever done was like having my fate determined by a lucky flip of a coin.

But, part of me knew that something was all wrong. My deepest feelings tugged at me from time to time, reminding me of the bright future Dad had once made me believe in. I longed for that sense of life, yet I was afraid of the disappointment that always seemed to crush any happiness I was able to find. At least I was free and, with my return to school, there was hope that I could put my life back on an even keel.

Because my car was still in need of work, I sold it for junk. That meant Mom had to trudge up and down the hill to the Merchandise Mart to go to work, which would be nearly impossible for her when winter came. She bought me another car, with the condition that it wouldn't be another clunker. I found a 1954 Mercury that I thought was beautiful. It was yellow with a black top and cost about $400. I was thrilled to have such a snazzy car.

I was also elated about the 1960 baseball season. As the summer unfolded, my Pittsburgh Pirates had come of age. They were in first place and held a comfortable lead over the Milwaukee Braves by the time I started tenth grade at Mt. Pleasant High. They never faltered and won the National League pennant. They would face the mighty New York Yankees in the World Series. Powered by Micky Mantle and Roger Maris, the Yankees were heavily favored to beat the Pirates. Mantle had led the American League with 40 home runs and Maris hit 39. The entire Pirate team hit only 120 homers.

As baseball experts predicted, it was a lopsided series with the Yankees scoring twice as many runs as the Pirates. Three of the games were complete blowouts with the Yankees winning by scores of 16-3, 12-0 and 10-0. Yet, after six games the series was tied at three games each. Game seven took place on Thursday afternoon, October 13. When school let out the Pirates were behind 7-4 going into the bottom of the eighth. They rallied for five runs to take the lead, but the Yankees tied the score at nine in the top of the ninth.

I was driving home when Pirate second baseman Bill Mazeroski stepped to the plate. And then the most incredible thing imaginable happened. Mazeroski hit a home run to end the game and made the Pirates world champions! I leaned on my '54 Merc's horn to celebrate my team's incredible victory. To this day, that is the most exciting and memorable moment I ever experienced as a baseball fan.

My elation over my new car and the Pirates' World Series heroics didn't last long. Geometry was as tedious as the first time around. The year off from school hadn't helped either. For the first time in my life I was struggling in my studies. I made matters worse by staying out late every night and drinking with my friends. It's hard to do well in school with a hangover, which I suffered from far too frequently. By December I was very depressed and, for the second time in a little more than a year, I decided to give up on education. I quit school again.

Within a week of quitting school several friends and I were arrested, each of us charged with possession of alcoholic beverages by a minor. For my friends, it was of no great consequence. For me, it meant another trip to the Workhouse unless I could post $1,000 bail. I had violated my probation and I would have to appear before a judge to see if my probation would be revoked.

CHAPTER 4. DESTRUCTION

Figure 4.2: *My biggest thrill in baseball was the ninth-inning home run by Pittsburgh Pirate second baseman Bill Mazeroski that clinched the 1960 World Championship.*

For the third year in a row, Christmas was just another day. That's the way most inmates view Christmas — just one more day to mark off of a calender. I begged Mom to find the money to pay a bail bondsman so I wouldn't have to spend another holiday season in jail. It wasn't until January that she finally put enough money together to bail me out.

The only things that mattered to me at this point in my life were baseball, my car and drinking with my buddies. Since the baseball season hadn't started yet, my friends and I spent most of our time driving around in our cars and drinking. To avoid being stopped by the Delaware police, we started spending most of our time just across the Pennsylvania, Maryland and New Jersey borders. It was also much easier to "get served" since bartenders in these neighboring states were usually far more lax regarding proof of age than they were in Delaware. But, as I would soon learn, this wasn't always true.

In late March we drove to Washington DC where the legal drinking age was eighteen. The first bar we went to refused to serve me. As I left, I smashed my fist through the bar's door window and ran down the street. Someone down the street smashed his fist into my face. When I woke up, I was in the hospital receiving stitches to close the gash under my eye. When the doctor finished, bandages covered my nose and my left eye.

I was arrested by the Washington police and sent to a detention center awaiting my probation officer who would come to Washington and return me to Delaware. I had to wait three days for him to pick me up. I kept to myself, reading a book about the final days of World War II in Germany.

For some reason, the black boys in the detention center decided they didn't like me. I overheard them talking and heard one of them say he wanted to "shut the other eye." I noticed that the guards were distracted and several boys were coming toward me. It was reminiscent of that day in Louisiana when I was going to get beat up for being a "yankee," only this time it was probably because these boys had me pegged as a "rebel." And, suddenly, an incredible thing happened.

"Wilcox, your probation officer is here," called a guard. A timely twist of fate had again spared me a pointless beating.

——— • ———

It was April 3, 1961 and I faced Judge Charles L. Terry, Jr. Our family lawyer, Hiram Warder, sat at my side as Judge Terry made his decision. With two counts of probation violation so

CHAPTER 4. DESTRUCTION

close together, there wasn't much doubt about what his decision would be.

"Probation is hereby revoked. The prisoner is committed for a period of two years at the New Castle County Correctional Institution," Judge Terry declared.

As I rose to be escorted out of the courtroom, Hiram Warder looked at me sadly and said something that sent chills up and down my spine.

"They don't care about rehabilitating you David, they just want to protect people from you."

———•———

That evening as I lay in the bunk of my six foot by nine foot prison cell after the lights went out, my mind was in turmoil. In a couple days I would be transferred to the First Offenders Building where I would have to stay for at least a year — well, provided I stayed out of trouble and made parole. Darting from one thought to another, almost at random, I took inventory of what my life amounted to. I was haunted by Hiram Warder's final words to me.

"They don't care about rehabilitating you David, they just want to protect people from you."

"What have I become?" I thought. My life had spun out of control. For the past three years I had spent as much time being locked up as I had spent on the streets. And now — more than at any time before — I understood why. I had turned into a menace, a person who couldn't stay out of trouble — a person people had to be protected from.

"They don't care about rehabilitating you David, they just want to protect people from you." I couldn't get Hiram Warder's words out of my head.

For the fourth year in a row I would be behind bars when Christmas came around. To my friends it had become a joke. One friend coined the phrase, "Keep the 'cox in Christmas." It didn't seem so funny any more, especially since the court wanted to protect people from the possibility that I might do something to ruin their Christmas.

"They don't care about rehabilitating you David, they just want to protect people from you."

And what about my so-called friends? How many times had they snitched on me to get the police to cut a little slack for them? My friends were part of the reason I wasn't even good at doing the things people needed to be protected from. I was probably the world's worst criminal. I had been caught for nearly everything of consequence I had ever done to break the law. And the primary reason I was in this cell was for a stupid string of break ins that put less than twenty dollars in my pocket. I certainly wasn't profiting from my crimes, yet people still needed to be protected from me.

I began to cry and covered my head with my pillow so nobody would hear. It did nothing to silence the deafening words echoing in my head, "They don't care about rehabilitating you David, they just want to protect people from you."

The early part of my life had been centered around Dad. Our closeness from as early as I could remember up to our wonderful trip to California in 1954 suddenly didn't seem so long ago. Route 66 had been a road leading to happiness and joy — the opposite of the hopeless road I was now traveling. I remembered that ten-year-old boy and how full of hope he had been. He certainly hadn't hoped to be a monster people needed protection from.

"They don't care about rehabilitating you David, they just want to protect people from you."

CHAPTER 4. DESTRUCTION

After I had left Dad's home a day early to go back to Bellefonte, he had said to me, "I wish you could have at least said goodbye to Peggy — she was very hurt." He only expressed concern for his loved one. He never mentioned how hurt he must have felt. It must have been devastating to him that the boy he had loved so intensely didn't want to be near him. We had so much in common. I had inherited his mind, his mathematical ability — much more so than my brother and sister had. It had been our common bond, the foundation of our love and of my devotion to him. That six-year-old boy who had announced, "Dad, I know what I want to be when I grow up — I want to be a scientist," had changed. That boy was growing up to be someone people had to be protected from.

"They don't care about rehabilitating you David, they just want to protect people from you."

How different I was from that boy who had always wanted to be a scientist! I would certainly not be able to become a scientist if I kept winding up in jail. A scientist needs an education. I had already dropped out of high school twice. Even if I went back to school and stayed out of jail, I would be two years behind. Would any college accept a person who dropped out of high school twice? Would they just laugh if I asked for financial support? Would any college want to take a chance on a young man that people had to be protected from?

It was like Hiram Warder was screaming at me as loud as he could, "They don't care about rehabilitating you David, they just want to protect people from you."

I had no one to turn to. Mom was not a source of inspiration. She was absorbed in her own misery — a great deal of which I had caused. I felt bad for her. She seemed to love me, but she was in no position to help. And, even when I did something right, she never seemed to notice. "Maybe," I thought, "even Mom needs to protected from my constant screw ups and all the grief I've brought to her."

"They don't care about rehabilitating you David, they just want to protect people from you."

For so long I had thought that, because the rule makers didn't follow their own rules, I had no obligation to be constrained by those rules. In my case, the rule makers were right. I had turned into something that people had to be protected from.

It was as though a small point source of light formed in the center of my mind with brilliant rays beaming in all directions, exploding into a tremendous flash — a flash that made everything clear. In that moment I understood precisely what I had become. I was a terrible person. I saw at once why society had given up on me. I was a loathsome creature that people no longer cared about. I hated myself at that split second because I completely understood far more than Hiram Warder ever could have imagined when he said, "They don't care about rehabilitating you David, they just want to protect people from you."

"I have to change, I have to change, I have to change," I sobbed as I cried myself to sleep. At the moment my troubled mind slipped from consciousness, the boy who had given in to hopelessness and despair — the boy who society had to be protected from — ceased to exist.

Chapter 5

Redemption

> *People are always blaming their circumstances for what they are. I don't believe in circumstances. The people who get on in the world are the people who get up and look for the circumstances they want, and if they can't find them, make them. – George Bernard Shaw*

There's something special about waking to the sound of birds chirping and singing. It's easy to imagine the busy mother bird feeding her babies, making sure their nest is both comfortable and safe, and perhaps even kissing her mate. I could hear their songs echoing through the building from somewhere above my cell, probably near the roof of the building. They were undoubtedly attracted by the warmth of the prison building that sheltered them from Delaware's cold April nights. Their happy sounds made me think of purpose, happiness and the joy of being alive.

My life had been like that once. I remembered a time when each new day brought a new adventure, when learning was my passion, when happiness was taken for granted and when I was filled with hope. I lay for some time with my eyes closed listening to the birds singing. I was at peace with myself and I decided to let the moment last before I started work on the big job I was about to undertake — the reclamation of my life.

It was as if Hiram Warder's damning statement had brought the ghosts of Christmas past, present and future to visit me in April. Like Scrooge in the Dickens' classic *A Christmas Carol*, I had seen the joy of my youth, my miserable existence of the present and my bleak prospects for the future. And, as with the fictional Scrooge, I was determined to alter the future I had seen.

When I woke up on the morning of April 4, 1961, I was a completely different person from the immature, belligerent, self-pitying boy who had fallen to sleep the night before in that prison cell. My name was still Dave Wilcox, but the similarity ended there. The nightmare that had begun in 1956 and persisted for five years had ended when the boy who people had to be protected from had fallen asleep.

I woke up as a young man realizing that I had left that boy behind. I felt like I had entered a universe from which the concepts of fear and pain had been obliterated. Those things had been replaced with certainty about what I had to do to change, the way I was going to make the change and with an acute awareness of an enemy I would have to guard against. While I had made my decision to change in the span of a single night, it wasn't really as sudden as it might seem. It was a decision I had postponed through all of the days since Dad died. I had chosen a hedonistic lifestyle to ease the pain of my anger over losing him, and it had led me directly to my prison cell.

There was no need to ask myself what and how I needed to change, the answer was obvious. I had to return to being the boy my dad had raised. I needed to return to the values he taught me, most importantly to always pursue the truth, to always be honest and to face the world with confidence. Everything else

CHAPTER 5. REDEMPTION

would follow from the basic principles Dad had emphasized. I was reaffirming a vow it had never really been necessary to take, because I had always known that it was the only proper way to live on earth. The first step in this process, of course, was to finish high school and find my way to college.

I knew I would have to go it alone. Everybody had given up on me, and who could blame them? I would have to become the master of my own destiny in a way that was constructive rather than being hell bent on destroying myself. I would have to depend on my own judgment and not rely on others, especially the budding con men and thugs I had surrounded myself with. It was the first time in my life that I truly understood the concept of self reliance.

I also knew I would have to fend off the naysayers of the world who do such a terrible disservice to young people — the wizened cynics who warn against setting goals too high with stupid clichés like "don't bite off more than you can chew." Dad had warned me about them. Because I had faced so much disappointment, I would have to be careful to avoid becoming discouraged when things didn't go as I hoped — it sure wouldn't help if I became a pessimist. I had a long way to go to straighten my life out, after all, and I had no certainty whatever that I would succeed. But then again, I was the person who figured out how to dig out from a bad situation the day I hit the grand-slam home run at Ferris that fired up the team. I wasn't sure how I would deal with setbacks and negative influences as I began my new journey, but I was confident I would think of something.

As I focused my mind on what I had to do to begin my new life, the first step was obvious. I had to get my education back on track, and I knew exactly how I was going to do it. I remembered that, not long after I had quit high school in December of 1960, I met a friend's sister. She was beautiful, smart and, because math came so easily to me, she thought I had potential to do a lot better in life than I was. She told me she would date me on the condition that I did something about getting an education. She suggested I look into International Correspondence School (ICS) and consider giving them a try. I discussed the idea with Mom and she pointed out that one of their most famous graduates was TV personality Arthur Godfrey, which was a "feather in their cap." Mom agreed with my new girlfriend and quickly turned to Aunt Isabel for the money to pay for the correspondence course. I had started it right before my fateful trip to the bar in Washington DC that had led to my two-year sentence.

I asked to see the prison's education director and he granted me an immediate audience. His name was Salerno, and I recall that he had dark bushy eyebrows and a pleasant disposition. I explained about the correspondence course and asked him to contact Mom so she could get all of the course material to me. He was familiar with ICS and said he would be happy to give me any assistance I needed. Since all letters from inmates had to go through a censor, he said he would handle my correspondence with ICS. This would avoid unnecessary delays.

Bingo! I accomplished the first step of my developing plan of action almost effortlessly thanks to the cooperation of this tough but compassionate prison official.

I was soon transferred to the First Offenders Building and the course arrived. The ICS books were very good and their tests were challenging. The first subject I studied was English and I found it quite interesting. Unlike the boring classes I had attended in public school, the course was arranged in a logical manner and it held my interest. It also helped that I wasn't spending the evenings cruising around the streets and getting drunk.

CHAPTER 5. REDEMPTION

Everyone in the First Offenders Building had a job. My first job involved scraping the varnish off of old chairs so they could be refinished. The work was boring and, far more importantly, it kept me away from my correspondence course. When the job of cleaning the visiting room became available, I was very interested. Somehow I lucked out and the job was mine.

I quickly realized that if I could be permitted to stay in the visiting room in the afternoons after I finished cleaning it, I would be free of all disturbances. Having my own personal place to study would be a godsend. I visited with Education Director Salerno again and asked him if he could help me get special permission to use the visiting room as what he said would be my own personal "study hall." He was amused and agreed to convince the First Offenders Building people to grant me permission. He concluded our meeting with a prediction. "You'll be all piss and vinegar for about a month, but I'm not sure your determination will last." When I left him, I distinctly remember thinking that I viewed his words as a challenge to me — and that I was determined to prove him wrong!

I decided to up the ante in facing Salerno's challenge. I selected my old nemesis as the next course I would tackle: plane geometry. I worked on it all through the summer of 1961 and mastered every aspect of the subject. The ICS book was outstanding, much better than the watered-down books that P. S. du Pont and Mt. Pleasant had used. I found geometry to be different from algebra but, in contrast to my earlier half-hearted tries, I discovered that it was every bit as challenging and fascinating. I saw that it would be useful as I moved on to more advanced math courses, especially the laws of logic that geometry makes extensive use of. When I finished the course, I thought, "Gee, I still have lots of piss and vinegar left." I had just discovered what my answer would be to anyone who said I was aiming too high: "You'll need binoculars to see how high I go!"

My confidence was growing as I completed each new course. Because I was studying five or six hours every day, I was able to make very rapid progress. Physics and American history took about a month each. By the end of September I was nearing completion of tenth grade.

Many of my friends from reform school and my old neighborhoods were doing time at the First Offenders Building. Observing me working with purpose probably convinced them that what I was doing was good — I can't recall any discouraging remarks. On weekends, I played softball and lifted weights; I was good at both. I could still hit a softball farther than most, even guys who weighed fifty pounds more than me. As in reform school, being a good athlete earned me the respect of other inmates who otherwise might have harassed me.

While learning was my number one obsession, I still took time out to follow Major League Baseball. Pitching-staff troubles had plagued my Pirates, but there was still something exciting to root for. Roger Maris and Mickey Mantle of the Yankees were both challenging Babe Ruth's single-season home run record. Mantle suffered an injury, which ended his chance of breaking the record. But Maris kept going, defying predictions of people who I came to regard as cynics and naysayers who said he couldn't do it. Finally, on October 1, 1961, I watched him hit his sixty-first home run on the First Offenders Building television. I took great personal satisfaction from seeing underdog Maris prove the cynics wrong.

As I would learn later, one of the lifers, Alex, decided that the visiting room job should go to another young boy in the First Offenders Building. The boy was his homosexual lover, or "punk" in prison jargon. He knew, of course, that I would not relinquish

CHAPTER 5. REDEMPTION

Figure 5.1: *Roger Maris meeting with President John Kennedy after hitting sixty-one home runs in 1961 to break Babe Ruth's single-season home run record. Maris gave me inspiration by defying the cynics and naysayers who said he couldn't do it.*

the job to anyone because it was so crucial to my studies. Since I had at least six more months to serve, he needed to find a way to have me removed from the job. One evening, there was a big disturbance in the dormitory on the second floor of the First Offenders Building. Pillows and blankets were thrown all over the place and inmate storage lockers were knocked over. Nothing was stolen or destroyed; it was just a big mess. Alex and several witnesses swore that I was the ring leader in the commotion that had taken place.

I was downstairs watching television, oblivious to what was happening. I denied having anything to do with what had transpired, which was the truth. But, because Alex was a "model inmate" and commanded the respect of prison authorities, they believed him. My punishment was to be sent to the "big house" to serve the rest of my term. This, of course, made my visiting-room job available for Alex's "punk."

I again turned to Education Director Salerno. I swore to him that I had nothing to do with what had occurred and that I didn't even know that it was happening. I'm sure he believed me. All I wanted from him was to get me excused from any jobs so that I could stay in my cell and study every waking hour. He smiled and said, "I'll put in a special request on your behalf and I'm sure they'll okay it." I had earned his respect and I felt proud.

I had also learned another lesson — I had learned that when I was faced with a bad break, with a little thought I could devise a course change and turn that bad break into a major stride forward. Many years later I would read about how many successful people indeed turn their disasters into new opportunities.

Instead of being depressed about losing my First Offenders Building visiting-room job and the excellent studying environment it provided, I was excited about being able to study from dawn to dusk. It accelerated my progress dramatically. I was ready to begin eleventh grade and I turned to second-year algebra. As usual, I found the ICS textbook and tests to be outstanding. It took me just four weeks to cover the subject.

It took less than two weeks each to cover courses such as biology, chemistry, eleventh-grade English and economics. It was January of 1962 and I was nearing completion of eleventh grade. I decided to move on to twelfth-grade math, which proved to be a snap. I completed trigonometry in three weeks and solid geometry in two weeks. I had now completed all of high-school math and was actually a year ahead of my contemporaries. I was sending my completed tests to ICS almost every day. They, in turn were sending the results to Charles Bomboy, Principal of Mount Pleasant High School.

Charles Bomboy was one of the old-time high-school principals for whom I had a great deal of respect. He had once caught a

CHAPTER 5. REDEMPTION

friend and me in a drug store having a soda rather than attending class, grabbed both of us by the hair and led us all the way back to school. He was a balding man with a thin nose that resembled a hawk's beak. A compassionate fellow who tried to help troubled school-age boys and girls who lacked interest in school, he had always taken a special interest in boys from broken homes like me who had gotten into trouble. That's the reason I had selected him as the person who would receive results of my ICS tests and final grades. I had chosen wisely!

"Wilcox, you have a visitor," the prison guard called out as he opened my cell door. It wasn't visiting day on this cold morning in February and I had no idea who it could be. My heart probably skipped a beat when I arrived in the visiting room and saw who it was. Charles Bomboy sat on the other side of the glass pane and he was smiling.

After exchanging greetings, he got right down to business. He told me he had followed my progress with ICS and was especially impressed with my accelerated pace. He explained that in order to receive a high-school diploma from Mt. Pleasant I could only get credit for one year from a correspondence course, even though I had completed tenth and eleventh grades plus some of twelfth. He pointed out that this was not a real problem provided I made parole in April. I would then be able to return to school and get credit for eleventh grade at Mt. Pleasant as though I had been there for the entire year. He told me that the only thing I was lacking was a foreign language course and that I should pick one and have ICS send the appropriate text.

"I've made arrangements with Mr. Salerno to have you take the SAT exams in March," Bomboy said. "He'll take you to P. S. du Pont to take the exams. This will tell me how well you've learned from the correspondence course."

Before our visit ended, I asked him about a university whose name I kept seeing in the newspapers, namely, the Massachusetts Institute of Technology or MIT for short. I read everything I could about America's developing space program, and there always seemed to be a quote from someone at MIT.

"The Massachusetts Institute of Technology," he told me, "is one of the best, if not the very best, engineering schools in the world."

"Then that's where I want to go to college," I told him.

Obviously amused by my bold statement, he said, "We'll see. But first things first. Get to work on a language right away and take the SAT tests. We'll talk about college when you get back to Mt. Pleasant in April."

This was incredible! I had sent him a couple of letters asking about the possibility of getting back into school, and he had answered with polite letters encouraging me to "keep up the good work." But nothing he had written gave any indication that he was planning something like this. All of my hard work had paid off. I had regained the confidence of this wonderful man who had tried so hard over the years to help me. Charles Bomboy was my number one supporter and he was a man who had the power to make things happen to help me. And, to top it off, he hadn't said anything to discourage me from setting my sights on a goal as high as going to MIT!

I followed Bomboy's instructions and ordered a course in French. As usual, the ICS book was outstanding and I quickly mastered the material. My teachers would eventually marvel at how perfectly I had mastered the pronunciation of French words, especially since I did it with no detectable accent.

While I awaited my special trip to P. S. du Pont to take the SAT exams, I had a visit from two of my Wilmington buddies,

CHAPTER 5. REDEMPTION

Figure 5.2: *Charles Bomboy in 1963. He went far beyond his call of duty as a high-school principal to help me.*

Tom and Jim, both of whom were college freshman. Tom had chosen the University of Maryland to study electrical engineering and Jim had opted for Temple University to study chemistry. Tom had attended military school, which had assured that he would stay out of trouble. I had actually helped Jim stay out of trouble by introducing him to one of the girls in my typing class back at P. S. du Pont. He spent most of his time with her rather than drinking with the guys and would eventually marry her. When I told them that I had chosen MIT as my college, they laughed. I just smiled and thought, "binoculars won't be enough, they're going to need a telescope to see how high I'm going."

When SAT exam day in March came, Education Director Salerno drove me to P. S. du Pont High. I took the three-hour test, which included a verbal part and a math part. The verbal part was difficult for me and I didn't think I had done very well. But, the math part of the exam had been almost trivial. There were only a few problems that gave me any difficulty.

My scores arrived in the mail, confirming my qualitative evaluation of how I had done. The scores on the SAT range between 200 and 800. I had scored only 428 on the verbal part, which was pretty low relative to most students who go to college. However, I scored 725 on the math part, which was good enough to get me into any college in the world.

And that world once again held potential for adventure and happiness. Each morning as I awoke to the purity of the morning light, I realized how much my fortunes had changed since I had chosen to live as a rational person. That choice had brought back hope for the future and certainty that I would never go back to the nightmare that landed me in jail. The certainty was based on the commitment I had made to living a clean life. Although I would not be able to name what I had done for another two years, I had adopted an objective moral code for which Dad had laid the foundation and that I would fine tune as I approached manhood. All I needed now was to regain my freedom.

The path back to freedom was through the parole board. With regard to education, I had done something that was certainly unprecedented by any inmate the board had ever heard of. I had not been in any fights, in large part because my older white friends and my black pals told their friends to leave me alone. They had, in effect, protected me both in the First Offenders Building and in the big house. But, I had one bad mark against me that held potential to prevent my making parole. I had been found

CHAPTER 5. REDEMPTION

unsuitable to remain in the First Offenders Building because of the disturbance I had been framed for.

On the day of my hearing I sat in a chair facing the parole board. The members seated were at a long table facing me. As I recall, they asked only two questions.

The first question dealt with how I felt about the crimes I had committed and if I felt I had been rehabilitated. Somberly, I recounted what I had realized the first night in my cell, and how Hiram Warder's words, "They don't care about rehabilitating you David, they just want to protect people from you," had made everything clear to me. I also focused on how hard I had worked to educate myself and how I wanted to continue on to college.

The second question dealt with the First Offenders Building disturbance. I assured them that I had been innocent of what happened that night. I stressed that if I had done what I had been punished for I would admit it. "I truly believe that lying is wrong," I concluded, "and I wouldn't want to begin my new life by telling one."

The vote was unanimous, I would be released on parole after completing one year of my two-year sentence. On April 3, 1962, I returned home to Clifton Park Manor ready to take on the world with purpose, happiness and the joy of being alive.

Chapter 6

Hope

> *It concerns us to know the purposes we seek in life, for then, like archers aiming at a definite mark, we shall be more likely to attain what we want. – Aristotle*

It was wonderful to wake up early on April 4, 1962 in my Clifton Park bedroom knowing that I had a busy day ahead. It would be my first day back to Mt. Pleasant High and I was excited about what awaited me. I had more than an hour to shower and eat breakfast before I caught the school bus. I wouldn't be taking the bus for long because my '54 Merc was stored at a gas station across the street from Brittingham's Drugstore in Edgemoor, just down the hill from Clifton Park. I would pick it up after school and I could drive to school from then on.

I lay awake for a few minutes and reflected on Mom. Although she hadn't smiled much, she was obviously happy that I was home. I had told her all about my studies on visiting days, which she never missed. I suppose it was her determination to see me through all of the tough times that softened my view of her. While I was in the Workhouse, I had plenty of time to think about what had happened between her and Dad, and I had made my peace with both of them.

I understood how Mom must have felt when, in her eyes, Dad abandoned her and why, like so many women who have suffered a divorce, she had poisoned my mind against Dad. While it had been cruel to me, it also made her life far worse than it should have been. Happiness is the catalyst of purification, and as my view of life had evolved from severe depression and hopelessness to the pure joy of being, I would not contaminate that view by harboring anger for her mistakes of the past. I viewed her in a new light, to be sure. But, at most, I felt a need to guard against letting her pessimism and bitterness dampen my spirits. For the first time, I truly recognized how much stronger I was than she. I was determined to bring her comfort to whatever extent I could.

I also understood that Dad must have suffered a loveless marriage for many years because he didn't want to abandon me. It must have been a living hell for him to see how badly things had gone after the divorce and I wondered if it contributed to his death. I had completely analyzed and rejected the picture that Mom had painted of him. I now realized how precious a gift he had given me by forsaking drinking and laying the moral foundation that gave me the strength to change and, in fact, save my own life. On that morning, I felt as deep a love for Dad as I had when I was a young boy. His goodness and purity of soul was a truth I knew that morning and that I had always known. More than ever before, I was determined to honor his memory by continuing from where we left off in 1954. In that spirit, I was committed to becoming a scientist.

Charles Bomboy had instructed me to come straight to his office when I arrived at Mt. Pleasant. He was elated to see me — almost as much as I was to see him. After exchanging greetings he got right to the point. I never knew him to make small talk for long, and I liked that about him.

CHAPTER 6. HOPE

He told me my SAT math score had far surpassed his expectations. He had expected me to score about 600; scoring in the 700s meant I was very gifted in math. I pointed out that my verbal score was almost 300 points lower and he dismissed it, assuring me that I would almost certainly score higher once I got into a regular high-school English class.

When I asked about what I would be studying in math, he gave me an answer that I was thrilled to hear. He had placed me in Mt. Pleasant's most advanced math class. He told me the teacher in this class, Mr. Boucher, was one of the best he had ever met. I welcomed the challenge.

I was really proud when he concluded our meeting by saying, "Your classmates will have to catch up with you. They still have about two more weeks to go until they finish trigonometry."

———•———

Bill Boucher was my second great teacher. He would pick up where Dad left off as he guided me through eleventh and twelfth grades at Mt. Pleasant. I wouldn't learn until twenty-five years after my high school days that Charles Bomboy had met with Bill before my return to school and made a special request.

"David has recently lost his father," Bomboy told him, "and I want you to be a surrogate father for him." He explained my background, including the time I had spent in the Workhouse and the way I had redeemed myself. Bill agreed and, as I look back at 1962 and 1963, I became so close to him that he indeed was like a second dad.

I was awe struck when I entered Bill Boucher's class room. There was a gigantic slide rule mounted above the blackboard. Because so many of the students' parents worked for the DuPont Company and Hercules Powder Company, the school was very modern and had excellent scientific equipment and facilities.

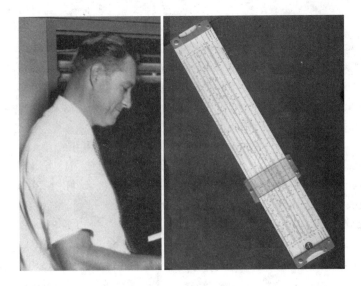

Figure 6.1: *My second great teacher, Bill Boucher, and the slide rule he taught me to use.*

Bill Boucher was thirty-seven and at the peak of his career. He was a handsome man with a wonderful smile and a terrific laugh. He was just what I needed, a mathematical whiz with a positive attitude and a man filled with confidence in his students — a lot like Dad. He would be a close personal friend long after I graduated from Mt. Pleasant High, so much so that I dedicated one of the books I have written to him.

In addition to being the school's top math teacher, he had a chess club and a hunting club, although I never joined either. He was also an entrepreneur who owned a miniature golf course and sold Christmas trees that he grew on his own property in Pennsylvania just across the Delaware state line.

He was not only my math teacher, he was my home-room teacher. The school day began in the home room where we spent

CHAPTER 6. HOPE

about an hour with him. Next was math class in the same room and then we went to our other classes the rest of the day.

Before I left for my next class on that first day, I asked Bill about solid geometry. He told me we would spend very little time on it because you can handle the subject much more easily using the techniques of calculus known as analytical geometry. And, to my great delight, he pointed out that we would actually start learning the basics of calculus before June and that we would spend an entire year learning differential and integral calculus in twelfth grade. He also noted that our textbook would be that of George Thomas, an MIT professor. He had not chosen to tell me this by accident — Charles Bomboy had apprised him of my desire to go to MIT. I sincerely doubt that either man ever advised students against biting off more than they could chew.

After my first day back to school I went to the gas station in Edgemoor to get my car. It was like greeting an old friend. My '54 Merc, in which I had heard the broadcast of Bill Mazeroski's 1960 World Series home run, was still beautiful to me even though it was filthy from sitting outdoors for a year. It took a while to get it started, but I soon had it running just fine. I drove it home and washed it in preparation for my second day of school.

I walked on air for the rest of the school year. I had learned well from ICS, especially in my two favorite subjects: math and physics. I did surprisingly well in French class, mainly because I had mastered pronunciation without ever having heard anyone speak in French. English and civics classes were better than I had remembered, but I was still a C student.

Bill Boucher made an unexpected and lasting contribution to my education in civics. In our home-room hour, Bill spent a lot of time talking about a man he thought would make an excellent president. The man was a Republican and his name was Barry

Goldwater. Bill correctly noted that we probably wouldn't hear Goldwater's name in our civics class. Political matters were of little consequence to me, so I didn't pay much attention at first.

When Bill asked me what I thought about politics, I told him my parents had always been Republicans, but I wasn't really very interested. He gave me a book to read entitled *Clichés of Socialism*, which discussed the fundamental premises of socialism. He wanted me to report back to him after I read it and tell him what I thought about the ideas the book discussed. It wasn't a very long book and I finished it in a couple days.

"I can't imagine how any sane person could be in favor of socialism," I told him. I was appalled by the horrible nature of a system that would pay an incompetent loafer the same amount it would pay a hard working innovator. I understood exactly why socialism would quickly kill ambition and ability. I rejected the premises of socialism because they run counter to the self reliance I had worked so hard to develop as my new way of life.

Bill was thrilled that I had learned so quickly and that I had given him the answer he was obviously hoping for. I started paying close attention to what he told us about the man he predicted would run against John F. Kennedy in the 1964 presidential election. My civics teacher laughed when I asked him why he only mentioned Nelson Rockefeller and George Romney when he discussed Republican presidential hopefuls and never included Barry Goldwater's name. Goldwater was too extreme he told me and didn't have a chance. From then on I made a point of injecting Goldwater's name in the class every time I could.

As a high-school junior, aside from the fact that he had been a Republican, I had no idea of what Dad's political views had been like. I wouldn't find out until much later in life when my brother Bob told me about Dad's dislike of Roosevelt, Truman

CHAPTER 6. HOPE

and just about any Democrat. I had no way of knowing that my surrogate dad, Bill Boucher, not only shared Dad's mathematical genius but his political views as well.

———   •   ———

In talking with the owner of the gas station where I had stored my car, I learned that a new Phillips 66 station had opened just across Governor Printz Boulevard and the owner had a job available for after-school work. It was just west of the Merchandise Mart next to the overpass that led to the DuPont Edge Moor plant. I introduced myself to the station owner, Bob Baker. We talked for a while and hit it off well. I was delighted when he hired me.

Baker ran a tight ship. When I waited on customers I had to sweep the car out and wash the windshield — even if the customer was buying fifty cents worth of gas! That was enough to buy two gallons in those days. He required me to do a complete inventory every time I shut the station down, which meant I counted every can of oil, every tire, etc. Finally, I had to do the books accounting for how much gas I pumped and whatever items I sold. It was really no big deal to me and I did my job flawlessly. Bob Baker was amazed that night after night my books balanced to the penny.

I was also balancing the merits of continuing to drive my '54 Merc. It really needed a paint job because of the year it had been exposed to the often inclement Delaware weather. And, its six-volt battery created a big problem in the winter. The voltage output of an automobile battery drops with temperature and, on very cold days, the car wouldn't start. The only way to counter the problem was to take the battery out of the car and bring it in the house overnight. I decided to look for a new car.

My friend Jerry had recently bought a great-looking car with a twelve-volt battery, and I decided I wanted the same model he had. They were available for $600 to $700, which was within reach of what I could afford, especially since my Mercury was in good shape and would bring at least $200 as a trade in. By the end of the summer I had saved enough to make a down payment on a beautiful maroon and white coupe with a four-barrel carburetor and dual exhausts that brought its V-8 engine up to 180 horsepower. Mom was pleased because it wouldn't cost her a cent, and all she had to do was co-sign for the loan. The best part of all was that I would be driving the car I had fallen in love with in Richardson Park when I was ten — a 1955 Chevrolet!

Figure 6.2: *When I entered my senior year at Mt. Pleasant High I would be driving the car of my dreams: a 1955 Chevrolet.*

Between having a job and dating a couple of nice looking girls from Mt. Pleasant High, I kept out of trouble, spending a lot of my spare time at the Kerry Drive-In on Governor Printz Boulevard three-quarters of a mile east of the Merchandise Mart. The Drive-In seemed like it was always packed with teenagers — it was the "in place" to go to meet friends and to pick up girls. And, it was a great place to show off a gorgeous '55 Chevy.

Only once did potential trouble come my way. One evening as closing time was approaching at the gas station, a carload of my old Wilmington buddies pulled in, fellows I had never really

CHAPTER 6. HOPE

liked very much. We talked for a while and the subject of stealing came up.

"Everybody who works in a gas station steals oil and stuff," one of them said.

"I don't," was my answer. I had come to regard Bob Baker as a friend, and stealing from him was unthinkable.

I thought they were making casual conversation. I didn't realize that they were feeling me out until they revealed their purpose. They asked me to leave a window in the back of the building unlocked so they could come back later and burglarize the station. I didn't have to think about my reply.

"There's no way I'll do that, get the hell out of here."

After they left, I thought about the implications of what they proposed. If I had agreed, I would have been an accomplice to burglary. If they had been caught, they would have blamed me and probably labeled me as the mastermind. That, of course, would have been a parole violation and an instant return ticket to the Workhouse. I called Bob Baker and told him about what had happened. He thanked me for telling him and said he would alert the police to keep an eye on the station. The next day I informed one of the potential burglars that I had alerted my boss to his plans and told him to stay away. I never saw any of them again and we were never burglarized.

Toward the end of the summer, there was an illness in Baker's family, perhaps his wife. During the illness, which lasted about two weeks, I was running the station full time. After he returned to work, it dawned on me that since I did my job with such perfection, I should ask for a raise over the $1.00 an hour I was earning. Confident that I was in a strong bargaining position, I told him I wanted $2.00 per hour and that, if he didn't agree, I was going on a one-man strike. Of course, I was his only employee.

He laughed and agreed to my terms. He never knew that I would have settled for $1.50.

——— • ———

When school started in September, I was a major sensation with the girls. My '55 Chevy was *the car* they wanted a ride home in. There were two or three girls I had driven home after school the year before in my '54 Merc, but now my car was packed from door to door. Every day I would take up a collection of the change the girls had left over from their lunch money. Some days they had as much as $1.00 and I would use it to buy some gas. Like the Merc, my '55 Chevy got ten miles per gallon around the city, so gas money was essential.

School was tremendous mainly because I was learning calculus, and learning it well. Ours was an exceptionally good class, better than any Bill Boucher had ever had before. It included Mt. Pleasant's two top students of 1963, a girl who would be the valedictorian and a boy who would be a very close runner up. Several of my classmates would eventually earn a PhD. I was enjoying it more than any class I had ever taken, and I even had the honor of teaching about what is known as l'Hôpital's rule, so named in honor of a French mathematician. I insisted upon calling it the "hospital" rule to show off my knowledge of French, which Bill Boucher found sufficiently amusing that he made me his substitute teacher for a day.

My teaching skills extended beyond the classroom. One of the eleventh-grade girls needed help in algebra and her father hired me as a tutor. I was really thrilled to discover that her father was the Honorable J. Caleb Boggs who had been Delaware's governor from 1953 to 1960.

One of the more amusing things that happened during my senior year took place in a bar. Not all of my P. S. du Pont friends

CHAPTER 6. HOPE

had gone afoul of the law. My friend Tom was now a sophomore at the University of Maryland and Jim was a sophomore at Temple University. I no longer drank on weeknights but, on Saturday evenings, Tom, Jim and I would team up with Jerry, my pal who had inspired me to buy a '55 Chevy. There was a bar near the Bancroft Mills in Wilmington that wasn't very diligent in checking for ID, and they would serve us without question.

Anyone in that bar who was close enough to hear our conversation must have thought we were crazy. Tom, Jim and I were all learning calculus and that's what we discussed, challenging each other's mastery of the subject. My high school class was comparable to their college classes, so I had no difficulty competing with them. Jerry had to bide his time during this phase of the conversation since he had not continued on to college.

Then, the conversation shifted to a more common topic of conversation in a bar — politics. Jim, who was Catholic, had been a big John Kennedy supporter in the 1960 presidential election. He had since changed his mind and thought Barry Goldwater would make a much better president. Tom and I agreed, and we explained our point of view to Jerry and anyone else within earshot. Bill Boucher would have applauded the conversation and would have been horrified about where it was taking place!

One of the barmaids would often join in. She was a refugee from one of the countries behind Russia's iron curtain, and she thought Kennedy and the Democrats were soft on communism. One evening, she handed me a slip of paper with the title and author of a book she recommended that I read — *Atlas Shrugged* by Ayn Rand. I put it in my wallet, figuring that I would go to the library and borrow the book when I found a little extra time.

Another interesting event was a presentation I attended at Mt. Pleasant detailing how scientists had discovered that, if you use liquid helium to cool a metal such as copper to a temperature near absolute zero, its electrical properties change dramatically. The metal exhibits no resistance whatever to the flow of electrons. Another thing I learned from the presentation was that such a material could actually block a magnetic field. I had just discovered the component needed for Dad's electric motor!

I suggested to my chemistry teacher, Vincent Remcho, that I build a physically possible version of Dad's motor and enter it in a science competition. Since I was one of his best students he agreed and said he would get me some liquid helium. Impressed by what I wanted to do, he also submitted my name as a candidate for the Bausch and Lomb Science Award. When he discovered how expensive and dangerous it would be to work with liquid helium, he decided the project wasn't feasible. But the award was feasible, and I was the 1963 winner at Mt. Pleasant High.

When the issue of selecting a college came up, my mind was already made up. I wanted to go to MIT. Bill Boucher and Charles Bomboy both agreed that I was an MIT caliber student. They thought it would be worthwhile for me to apply to at least one other college. Carnegie Institute of Technology in Pittsburgh had a scholarship competition, so I felt it would be a reasonable alternative if I couldn't find a scholarship to go to MIT. They were the only two colleges I would apply to.

However, it wasn't clear how good my chances of being accepted by either school were. As Charles Bomboy had predicted, I had brought my SAT verbal score up to 554 and even improved my math score by twenty points. But, the combined score was borderline for both universities. Also, my quilt work high-school education and the C's in courses other than math and science gave me roughly a B average. I would need something to get the colleges' attention to convince them that they should accept me.

CHAPTER 6. HOPE

I found that something in January of 1963. There was a second type of SAT exam that measured how much a student had learned, as opposed to the aptitude exams I had taken that measured ability. In 1963, they were called "achievement" exams, and today they are known as SAT II. Bill Boucher had advised our math class to take the math achievement test as a trial run just before we finished eleventh grade. I had made an outstanding 759, just 41 points short of a perfect score. If I could improve on that score, I hoped it might be enough to get me into MIT.

On SAT exam day, I breezed through the test — I had been uncertain about only one of the problems. Consequently, I had expectations of doing a little better than I had done the year before. When I received my test score, it was another magic moment of success and accomplishment that sent a flock of butterflies directly to my stomach — something that was becoming a habit since I had awakened in a prison cell determined to change my life. I had scored a perfect 800!

"That 800 will get you into MIT," Bill Boucher predicted.

I applied to MIT and Carnegie Tech and hoped for the best. Pointing out that I was a straight-A student in math and science and had made the highest possible score on the math achievement test, both Bill Boucher and Charles Bomboy thought my chances of getting into MIT were excellent.

Success was becoming commonplace for me. There seemed to be no limit to the opportunities that life presented, and I was amazed how much difference a year had made. Just a year ago I was still sitting in a prison cell hoping that all of my hard work would pay dividends, and that I could at least finish high school. Now my sights were set on something much higher. I decided to formulate a set of three goals that, as it turns out, would play a significant role in shaping my life.

Goal One was not only to go to school at MIT, but to earn my Bachelor's degree in three years as well. That would make up for the year I had lost by quitting school twice.

Goal Two was to continue beyond a Bachelor's degree to the highest degree possible — a PhD — and to earn it with six total years of college. The six-year part of the goal was inspired by a man who spoke to our calculus class — I think he may have been from computer giant IBM. He talked about college and what it was like. I asked him how quickly it was possible to go from a high-school diploma to a PhD. His answer was that six years was possible for a student who really worked hard.

Goal Three was to found my own business before I turned thirty. To some extent, this goal was stimulated by my exposure to Bill Boucher's entrepreneurial nature. I had read an article about how researchers had studied entrepreneurs to determine what they have in common. Education is not a common denominator, nor is ethnicity or any other factor, save one. They found that the primary thing entrepreneurs have in common is a parent who has been self employed — a parent like my dad. Working for myself was "in my blood," and Bill Boucher was reinforcing my predisposition to be an entrepreneur.

Charles Bomboy and Bill Boucher had been right. Both Carnegie Tech and MIT accepted me. The acceptance letter from MIT came first. If I had been driving, I would have leaned on my horn ten times longer than I had when Mazeroski hit his World Series clinching home run in 1960.

This was the world I had anticipated as a young boy before tragedy had temporarily intervened. It was a world I had regained through the power of ideas and through persistence, determination and earning the respect of people who recognize and respect those traits. It was a world in which my boldest dreams came true. It

CHAPTER 6. HOPE

was a world in which I awoke each morning with the same sense of excitement and energy that I had known in our Richardson Park home. It was a world in which I belonged.

———•———

It was June 13, 1963, and graduation day had finally arrived. I remember how happy Mom was, or perhaps relieved is a more apt description.

"I thought this day would never come," she said.

I remember thinking that her perspective was completely different from mine. I had told her about my three goals and she seemed indifferent to my big plans. I wasn't sure she even favored my going to college. I really didn't understand her at all — I saw my high-school diploma as a means to accomplishing my three goals. My focus was squarely on the future.

Being accepted at MIT meant I was on my way to accomplishing Goal Number One. There was plenty of work ahead to get through college in three years, of course. And a problem remained as I had not qualified for a scholarship. A week or two before graduation day, Charles Bomboy had told me not to worry about it because he would find the money to get me to MIT. Because I had heard nothing from him, I was concerned about my prospects. I had already looked into the possibility of finding a part-time job and going to the University of Delaware for a year. I thought that if I did real well I could convince MIT to take a chance on me. It wasn't much of a plan, but I was trying to take action to control my fate rather than waiting for others to do it for me.

About a week after graduation day, Charles Bomboy finally called and told me he had just spoken with a woman named Mrs. E. Paul du Pont. He explained that he had told her about how I had lost my dad when I was fourteen, the trouble I had gotten into and what I had done with my correspondence course at the Workhouse. He had explained to her that I was accepted at MIT but lacked the financial resources to be able to go.

He concluded by telling me what she said when he had finished explaining my situation to her. And what Charles Bomboy told me is something that will resonate in my mind forever.

He told me she had asked just one question. Her question told me how much is possible for a young man who works hard in America, especially in the face of adversity — even adversity of his own making, provided that young man realizes his mistakes and takes positive action to reshape his life. Her question told me that my group of guardian angels had grown from two to three: Mrs. du Pont now stood shoulder to shoulder with Charles Bomboy and Bill Boucher. When he told me what her question was, I felt the hair stand up on the back of my neck — it was the electrifying feeling of sheer ecstasy. Mrs. du Pont's question consisted of just five words.

"How much does he need?"

Chapter 7

The Bright Sun of Tomorrow

> *Press on — nothing can take the place of persistence. Talent will not; nothing is more common than unsuccessful men with talent. Genius will not; unrewarded genius is almost a proverb. Education will not; the world is full of educated derelicts. Perseverance and determination alone are omnipotent. – Calvin Coolidge*

Jean Kane Foulke du Pont was the granddaughter of William Foulke, discoverer of the first full dinosaur skeleton in North America. Born in 1891, she married E. Paul du Pont in 1910. Her husband was an American industrialist who founded DuPont Motors, which briefly manufactured automobiles.

Mrs. du Pont was, by all measures, a very progressive woman for her times. As a young woman, she was very active in America's women's suffrage movement. In 1916, for example, she was one of several Delaware women who picketed the White House in an attempt to influence President Woodrow Wilson to champion their cause.

By 1919 she found what would be her lifelong passion: prison reform. In that year she helped found the Delaware Prisoner's Aid Society and a detention home for juvenile offenders called Bridge House. Later on, she helped found Delaware's Family Court.

Charles Bomboy had contacted Prisoner's Aid in his quest for a scholarship that would cover my costs at MIT. They, in turn, put him in direct contact with Mrs. du Pont. He was certainly aware of her active role in helping people who had a genuine interest in rehabilitating themselves. He also knew of the scholarship fund she had that helped many students. Most important, he was certain that, because I had a foot in each of the areas she cared about, he could convince her that I was the quintessential example of the kind of person she wanted to help. That's why he told me not to worry about financial support for MIT.

Figure 7.1: *Mrs. E. Paul du Pont.*

She named her scholarship fund the *Theano Foundation*, after Greek mathematician Pythagoras' wife. She had chosen the name in honor of her husband who, she would tell me, knew many different ways to prove the famous Theorem of Pythagoras, one of

CHAPTER 7. THE BRIGHT SUN OF TOMORROW

the most important concepts in geometry. From the very beginning of my association with her, she always referred to me as her "number one scholar."

Because several members of the du Pont family had attended MIT, Mrs. du Pont had a great deal of insight about the school. Most important, as she would write in one of her letters to the bank official who administered the *Theano Foundation*, MIT was more like a "graduate school" than a regular undergraduate school. So, she concluded, she wanted me to attend summer school at the University of Delaware in order to properly prepare for the rigors of college life.

I took two courses at the University of Delaware in the summer of 1963: calculus and economics. I was a little disappointed with the fact that the school wouldn't let me take anything more advanced than their second-semester freshman calculus course. The mathematics-department official I spoke with seemed unwilling to accept the fact that a high school could possibly cover the same material that the University did in one year. Perhaps he thought I would be "aiming too high" by jumping all the way to sophomore-level calculus.

He was wrong and the calculus course I took covered material I had learned from Bill Boucher. But, it didn't matter. The summer course served two important purposes. First, I learned to take good lecture notes, something that is essential for doing well at any college. Second, I received credit for both courses at MIT, which gave me a head start on my plan to graduate in three years.

Another important thing happened during the summer. I recalled the slip of paper I had saved in my wallet that the barmaid had given me during one of my Saturday night political discussions with Tom, Jim and Jerry at the bar near the Bancroft Mills. I went to the Wilmington library and found that *Atlas Shrugged* by Ayn Rand was unavailable. It was in very high demand and was, in fact, spoken for all summer long. But, I learned, she had written three other novels, and I read all three.

I discovered that Rand was much more than a novelist, she was a philosopher. Hers was a philosophy, above all, about individualism and self reliance. Her philosophy constituted a strong code of moral values that were centered about truth, honesty and integrity. A refugee from Russian communism, Rand hated socialism and was the ultimate champion of free enterprise. Many conservatives like Barry Goldwater admired her for her clear thinking and positive ideas. A few conservative thinkers, most notably William F. Buckley, disliked her because she was an atheist — even though he agreed with her on just about everything else. Liberals, of course, hated her.

I was captivated by Rand's writing and her ideas. When I got to MIT, I bought a copy of *Atlas Shrugged* and discovered that it was the climax of her writing. It was the best novel I had ever read, and I understood why the Bancroft Mills barmaid had recommended that I read it. Most important, I now fully understood the enormous benefits that go hand in hand with following a good moral code and, perhaps even more significantly, how important it is to never deviate from that code. Telling even a "little white lie," for example, still makes you a liar. Rand's ideas on morality further reinforced what Dad had taught me.

——— • ———

MIT was awesome! It was also very intimidating. In reading about who my classmates would be, I discovered that one-third were valedictorian of their high-school class, their combined SAT scores were nearly 100 points higher than mine and their high-school grades were pretty close to an A average. Also, MIT took just one semester to cover what I had learned in calculus.

CHAPTER 7. THE BRIGHT SUN OF TOMORROW

Figure 7.2: *The "Great Dome" at MIT.*

That meant the work pace was twice as fast as the University of Delaware! I wondered if I could maintain even a C average with the kind of competition I would face.

On the positive side, the acceptance rate was only 10%, which meant MIT had decided I had more potential than 90% of the students who had applied for admission. Also, my math SAT score was higher than average for an MIT freshman. And I knew none of my classmates had scored higher than I had on the math achievement SAT exam.

It didn't take long to realize that MIT was tailor made for me. All but one of the courses I would have to take each semester would be science or math. Unlike most universities, the school put no limit on how many courses a student could take. MIT apparently felt the student should be the one to decide on how much he could "bite off and chew." This was my kind of place!

I started cautiously, taking the normal five courses. I made an A in calculus but, because I had taken the required humanities course and French, the C that I received in each gave me a grade point average that was slightly below a B average. I realized that if I always took an extra math course rather than a non-technical course like French, I could maintain better than a B average. My plan worked. I took six courses in the second semester — three of which were mathematics courses — and improved my grade-point average to well above the B level. This was an important breakthrough because I would have to take six courses each semester in order to graduate in three years.

When the school year ended I realized I had several things going for me that would be the key to my success at MIT. For one thing, I was a year older than my contemporaries and I was therefore a bit more mature. Also, I had purpose, namely to accomplish my goal of getting through in three years. Finally, I had learned how to study from early morning to late at night when I was working on my correspondence course. That was a tremendous asset since taking six courses each semester would require that kind of perseverance and determination.

I also learned that being an MIT student guaranteed that your head never swelled. It was because of those 180-IQ guys who always had the answers to homework and exam problems (physics in particular) that stumped us mere mortals. I had to study every day to keep pace, which meant drinking was out of the question, even on weekends. I had to work extremely hard to earn even a B in most of my courses, so every A was a major achievement. Attending MIT was truly a humbling experience because, as Mrs. du Pont had observed, it was essentially a graduate school masquerading as an undergraduate institution. If I had it to do over again knowing what I know now, I would still select MIT as my college as eagerly as I did the first time around.

Finally, I found that brilliant minds come in all races, creeds, colors and sexes. Yet, during the turbulent 1960s, many of the highly-intelligent people who were my MIT classmates would have had to sit in the back of buses in places like Lake Charles,

CHAPTER 7. THE BRIGHT SUN OF TOMORROW 117

Louisiana. I can't imagine a better cure for racism and bigotry than to spend a year at MIT competing for good grades!

My friend Tom from the University of Maryland visited me at MIT and we decided to drive to California and spend the summer there, assuming we could find jobs. The drive to California was sensational with Route 66 still being the primary road to California. Tom worked as a Fuller Brush salesman and I secured a job at Disneyland as a dishwasher for Aunt Jemima's kitchen. I tackled my job as though it were the most important job in the world. I was proud when my boss said, "You're the best dishwasher I've ever had."

The drive home was a real nostalgia trip. We visited Hoover Dam, the Grand Canyon, the Petrified Forest National Park and the Painted Desert — all of the places I had visited on the trip with Dad back in 1954. We also included a trip to Barry Goldwater's house and the Goldwater family store in Phoenix. Barry was busily campaigning for the presidency against Lyndon Johnson, who had ascended to the office after John Kennedy was assassinated in November of 1963. We took a couple of rocks from his driveway as souvenirs. Many years later, after I confessed in a letter to him about my "crime," Goldwater wrote me and said he "never missed the rock." He eventually autographed it for me.

Returning to MIT in the fall, I tackled the core courses that would lead to a Bachelor's Degree in pure mathematics. My overall average was again above the B level, which was sufficient to make the Dean's List, a distinction that put me in the upper third of my class. However, I was beginning to realize that I liked calculus and solving differential equations much more than most of my pure math courses. Calculus involved practical problem solving and pure math was more of an exercise in logic, a little like the contrast between high-school algebra and geometry. I decided to change my major subject to aeronautics and astronautics. I had no idea that Christmas vacation in 1964 was going to bring another major change in my life.

——— • ———

Born on March 19, 1947, Barbara Gagliardino was the second of Sabby and Rose Gagliardino's five children. The Gagliardinos lived in New Castle south of Wilmington within three miles of the Delaware Memorial Bridge that spans the Delaware River and provides a driving route between Delaware and New Jersey. Barbara was a pretty brunette with a world of talent and ability. In addition to having a sharp mind, she was a fine jazz dancer. Of pure-blooded Italian heritage, she graduated from high school in 1964 and was already keeping the books for the family bakery.

Barbara had a girlfriend who was dating a young man from Wilmington. The young man, in turn, had a friend who was home on Christmas vacation from college and he proposed that they go out on a double date. Barbara agreed to the blind date and hoped for the best.

That's how Barbara and I met. I was so enamored with her that it was difficult to breathe that night and for the days to follow. We kissed on that first date and it wasn't long before I knew I wanted to spend the rest of my life with her.

She wasn't as head over heels in love as I was, but I had an ally. Her mom, who everyone calls Rosie, was one of my biggest fans. She, in effect, told Barbara, "don't let that college kid get away." Rosie and I won out — Barbara and I decided that we would marry in June after the 1965 school year ended.

I told Mrs. du Pont about my plans and she was understandably concerned. How would this added responsibility affect her number one scholar? To find out, she insisted that Barbara and I have lunch with her during Easter vacation.

CHAPTER 7. THE BRIGHT SUN OF TOMORROW

When we arrived at her home in Montchanin, Barbara told Mrs. du Pont that her family name was Gagliardino. "Oh, you're Rosie's daughter!" she exclaimed. Mrs. du Pont's son had married the daughter of Rosie's next door neighbor — they had met over coffee many times. As we conversed, Mrs. du Pont confirmed her approval. Before we sat down for lunch, she told Barbara, "You're getting the short end in this marriage." She explained that life with a scientist is a real challenge for any woman.

I returned to school and my grades were the highest yet. I was on the brink of making the "Upper Dean's List," which was reserved for students with an average closer to an A than to a B — only about 10% of the class qualified. Best of all, it was now obvious that I would be able to graduate in three years provided I took two summer courses at MIT.

Barbara and I married on June 12, 1965. My brother Bob was my best man, and we had our wedding in New Castle. We were honored to have Mrs. du Pont as one of the people present while we took our marriage vows. Sadly, Charles Bomboy had passed away, a victim of cancer — it was a moment I wish I could have shared with him. The next day, we drove to Cambridge, Massachusetts so I could begin my summer courses at MIT. Because we had no time for a honeymoon, Mrs. du Pont treated us to a belated honeymoon at her vacation home on Block Island, Rhode Island during the long Fourth of July weekend in 1965.

Within three months after our marriage, we conceived our first child. When we told Mrs. du Pont, it added even more urgency to something she was concerned about. She knew that, because of my police record, I would have a difficult time getting a security clearance when I graduated and took a job with an aerospace company. A clearance was essential in those days. She also knew I wouldn't be able to vote because I had committed a felony. To eliminate these problems, she had been contemplating applying to Delaware's governor to grant me a pardon. She would eventually express the sense of urgency in a letter to the governor saying she didn't want the baby to ever have to "hang her head in shame" because of what I had done as a teenager.

Mrs. du Pont told me of her plan and asked if I knew a lawyer who could help. I immediately thought of Hiram Warder, and when I called him he agreed to handle all of the details. She was delighted to find out that she would be working with a man called "Hi" about whom she had heard so much, but had never met. He had been heavily involved with the Family Court system she helped create.

In mid-March I went to Delaware to have my pardon hearing. The most ironic part of it was that the man who would make the decision was the very man who had sentenced me to that two-year term in the Workhouse. Charles L. Terry, Jr. was now governor of the state of Delaware!

I don't remember much about the hearing other than a lame comment I made that wound up being printed in the newspaper. In answer to a question Governor Terry asked me, I said something about how we often have more than one road to choose in life and I had now chosen "the right road." My friends really jazzed me for not coming up with something more original.

On May 5, 1966, Governor Terry granted me a full pardon. He said in the pardon that "if there was ever a case in which a pardon was justified, this is the one." He made it clear that it wasn't just a pardon, it was a complete exoneration. He wanted me to embark on life "with a record free of blemish."

It was a wonderful day for Hiram Warder because of his long association with Dad and with me. He had accompanied me to all

CHAPTER 7. THE BRIGHT SUN OF TOMORROW

Figure 7.3: *Delaware Governor Charles L. Terry, Jr. granted me a pardon exonerating me for all of my transgressions. He was the same man who, as a judge, had revoked my probation and sent me to the Workhouse.*

of my court hearings, and he had helped Dad in his unsuccessful efforts to send me to *Boy's Town* rather than reform school. Yet, he felt nothing he had done had helped in any perceivable way — until now. Of course, I told him about the effect he had on me when he said, "They don't care about rehabilitating you David, they just want to protect people from you." But, for him, the pardon was something tangible he had done for me and for the memory of Dad. He and Mrs. du Pont had been a wonderful team. I realize today that he was my fourth guardian angel, and that he had actually been the first.

And, of course, Mrs. du Pont was elated. Her wish had come true because the baby had not yet been born. It was just in the nick of time because our daughter, Kinley, was born just three days later.

My final year at MIT was terrific; I made my best grades ever. I had planned so well that I only needed five courses in my final semester. I received an A in four of the courses and a B in the other — grades I could never have guessed I was capable of when I was just starting at MIT. I had actually received better grades at MIT than I had in high school and, of course, I accomplished Goal Number One!

——— • ———

In late June of 1966, Barbara and I moved to California where a job awaited me with Douglas Aircraft in Long Beach. This was yet another one of my childhood dreams come true. I had never forgotten my wonderful days in California with Aunt Isabel and her son Warren. This time I was coming to California to stay.

After working for a year at Douglas Aircraft, I was accepted for graduate study at the California Institute of Technology where I met my third great teacher, Dr. Philip Saffman. In addition to being a wonderful teacher and PhD thesis adviser, he told me that he felt a truly dedicated student should pursue his studies like a monk in a monastery. For students who did that, he added, six years from high school to PhD should be the norm.

In June of 1970, after just three years of study under the guidance of this brilliant mathematician/scientist, I graduated with a PhD in Aeronautics. I had accomplished the second of my high-school goals by earning a PhD with just six years of college.

While I was at Caltech, my son Robert Sabatino Wilcox — named after his two grandfathers — was born. The year was 1969. Dad would have been tickled to know that his grandson was born in the year that Neil Armstrong became the first man to walk on the moon.

After a brief time working for various Southern California aerospace companies, I founded my own company, which I named DCW Industries. The company came into existence on July 19, 1973. Since I was twenty-nine years old, I had accomplished

CHAPTER 7. THE BRIGHT SUN OF TOMORROW

my third goal. Initially focused on aerospace research, the company prospered and I have published more than seventy scientific reports and journal articles in some of the aerospace industry's most prestigious journals. The company now specializes in book publishing, and I have written several college-level textbooks that are used in universities all over the world.

Mom and I wrote each other from time to time until she passed away in 1977. In one letter she told me something that proved to be one of the nicest things she ever did for me. She told me that I had a relative who was a professor at UCLA. His name was Bill Meecham and he was my Aunt Mabel's son. Since Mabel was Dad's sister, we were first cousins.

I contacted Bill and discovered that we had more than our bloodline in common — we were both working in the same field! We became friends and he helped me obtain a part-time teaching job at UCLA in 1981. I have been a fixture in the Mechanical and Aerospace Engineering Department ever since.

When Aunt Mabel died in 1987, Bill showed me some genealogical information that was among her belongings. I noticed that Dad had a brother named Arthur who had died in 1947 when I was three years old. At the age of 43, I had just discovered that I had an uncle I was completely unaware of. Of even greater significance, this information revealed a great deal about my family roots dating back through ten generations in America.

The genealogical information had been compiled by Pauline Wilcox, who was the wife of Arthur's youngest son, Ralph. I learned that all but one of Uncle Arthur's children were alive, including Gene and Mary Wilcox who still operate the Wilcox family farm in Boyertown, Pennsylvania, just a few miles from Quakertown. I also learned of my ancestor Laban Landon who served as one of George Washington's bodyguards and Great Grandpa

Sevellon Wilcox, who served in the Union Army during the Civil War. In 1988 I met all of my cousins at a Wilcox family reunion in Quakertown.

———— • ————

Just over nine years passed from the day I woke up in a six foot by nine foot prison cell determined to reclaim my life to the day Caltech President Harold Brown handed me my Doctorate. I had taken a journey that required a great deal of hard work, some good fortune and the assistance of some wonderful people. Among those wonderful people, the gracious and generous Jean Kane Foulke du Pont stood out not only as a benefactor but, eventually, as a dear friend.

I visited with Mrs. du Pont just after I graduated from MIT in 1966 to thank her for all she had done for me. I offered to pay her back with installments over time so other scholars could get the kind of education she had made possible for me.

"Oh, heavens no," she said, "we wouldn't know how to handle it with the IRS."

She went on to tell me that I could repay her by making sure my children went to their college of choice. It wasn't much of a repayment I thought, because Barbara and I couldn't imagine doing otherwise.

I sent her a letter in 1986 to tell her that I had just fulfilled part of my promise to make sure my children received the college education they wanted. My daughter Kinley would be graduating from college almost twenty years to the day from when I had graduated from MIT. Sadly, a reply came back telling me that Mrs. du Pont had passed away.

But, over the years, I always felt that I owed her far more than what she had asked of me. Another seventeen years passed before I discovered a way to make the kind of repayment she deserved...

Epilogue

> *It is one of the most beautiful compensations of life, that no man can sincerely try to help another without helping himself.* – Ralph Waldo Emerson

"So what's the verdict Jim, did I ruin any possibility of running for public office back when I was a teenager?"

I held my breath as I waited for Jim Rogan to answer. I didn't have to wait long.

"First of all, Dave, I'm jealous of a guy who has a better story than mine. Second, why aren't you telling young men this story?"

"Jim, I've rarely spoken of my teen years over the past forty years. And I really mean it. You're only the third Californian I've told about what happened back in Delaware."

"Dave, it's a true American success story. It's really inspirational. You have nothing to be ashamed of. What you did as a seventeen-year-old boy proves that anything is possible in America if you work hard enough."

"I can see myself working with teenagers who've been in trouble. I've been a teacher for more than twenty years. But, what about running for the Assembly? Would I be an embarrassment to the Republican Party?"

"You'll be fine provided you present the story on your own terms."

"Okay Jim, I'm sold. I'll give it a try. If I can help others by telling them how I turned my life around, that's a good thing."

"You won't regret it Dave. Just imagine that many years from now you're sitting on a park bench and a young man walks up and tells you that you changed his life by telling him your story. If you save just one person you'll be a success."

My wife, Barbara, and I had agreed that I should seek Rogan's advice before taking a plunge into politics in a big way. Jim had been our Congressman. My son and I had worked in all four of his election campaigns, one for the California Assembly and three for the United States Congress. He knew me well. I had sent him email the day before outlining my days as a teenager.

We continued discussing the possibility of my becoming a candidate for the California State Assembly and I decided to postpone my decision for a while longer. It was mid-May of 2003 and the canyon view from my home-office window was dominated by a deep shade of green. Rogan's words made the Southern California sun a little brighter and the trees in the canyon just a bit greener.

I took immediate action on Rogan's suggestion that I try helping young people who had gotten in trouble. I realized that I had finally found the answer to the question I had posed to Mrs. du Pont so many years ago. I knew exactly how to repay her for putting me through college. I imagined how she might have responded had I suggested that I would repay her by helping young people who had gotten in trouble with the law by telling them how I overcame my own youthful mistakes. I'm sure she would have said, "Yes, David, you will repay me a hundred times over if you do that."

It didn't take very long to reach Ed Anhalt, a man who had been instrumental in establishing a series of "boot camps" for juvenile offenders in Los Angeles County. Ed was the Director at Camp Kenyon Scudder in Saugus. Located about an hour's drive north of Los Angeles, Camp Kenyon Scudder houses roughly 100 boys, ages thirteen to eighteen. I learned from the Camp's literature that most are there for less serious offenses, such as "violating probation after they were convicted of previous offenses ranging from burglary to car theft." How familiar that sounded! The Probation Department of Los Angeles County, which oversees the camps, authorized Ed to have me come to the camp so I could meet and work with some of the camp's teenagers.

Ed is a man just a tick under six feet tall whose build and poise tell you he is a man of action. While his face could be described as stern, the moment he relaxes into a smile you can't miss his warmth. He is a genuine person with great compassion for the boys under his supervision.

Ed selected six boys he thought I would have the biggest impact on. Four were of Hispanic descent and two were black. Each had expressed an interest in straightening himself out, finishing high school and going on to college.

I decided to first relate what I had gone through as a boy and how I had changed my life. I immediately got their attention. They recognized that my offenses were about the same as theirs, but that I had been incarcerated in a much worse place than Camp Scudder. They also knew that Caltech is unique and how much it means to earn a PhD from such a prestigious institution.

"Consider the contrast between my life before and after I realized I wanted to change," I told them. "The life I had chosen as a teenager would have led to disaster. While my crimes were minor, it's likely that I would have moved on to much worse things. There was a fellow a few cells from mine who I had seen often in my neighborhood. He was a member of a small gang that specialized in blowing safes. The leader was a young genius who knew a lot about chemistry. Maybe he would have liked having somebody with strong mathematical ability in the gang."

"A young black friend of mine had just been sentenced to seven years for armed robbery," I added. "That is another avenue I might have chosen. I was so angry and full of doom and gloom that I was wasting my mind by traveling a desperate and deadly road — wasting a mind capable of earning a PhD from Caltech."

"Everything I tried failed when I was getting in trouble and refusing to follow society's rules. All of this changed when I chose a life of honesty, integrity and hard work. It was like I flipped a switch and happiness replaced sadness, success replaced failure, confidence replaced fear and anxiety. I have faced some disappointment, of course, but it's really no big deal. I just look for ways to turn my disappointments into new opportunities — something I discovered while I was turning my life around."

"The most important thing I want you to remember about me is what made my change possible," I stressed. "It was the power of an idea — the idea that I could design a completely new course for my life and find a way to accomplish my goals. It all started with that single idea, and it has lasted a lifetime. You have, within yourselves, the power to do the same thing."

Over the next few weeks I had them read several chapters from Ayn Rand's *Atlas Shrugged*. I told them how, because it stresses the power of individualism and self reliance, the book had a profound effect on me as a young adult. The book is loaded with symbolism pertinent to their lives, and I was certain it would help them.

For example, in the early part of the book a character named Eddie Willers tells of a great oak tree that he had regarded as a great symbol of strength. One morning, after a storm, he notices that the oak had been struck by lightning. On inspecting the tree, he discovers that it had died long ago and was hollow inside — a lot like my teenage buddies who turned on me to get a break from the police — a lot like these young fellows' "homies." And, I pointed out to them, a lot like politicians, who are too often completely devoid of virtue.

I used other scenes in the book to demonstrate that their fate was not in the hands of others, but in theirs alone. While virtually all of these boys had never known his father, and didn't have a foundation laid in his early years comparable to mine, I reminded them that I had taken the initiative to save myself without the help or encouragement of anyone. Only after I had proven that I was serious about changing my life did others offer help. I stressed that each boy had the power to do the same. As evidence, I cited the fact that every boy agreed that he had decided to take complete charge of his life about the time he became a teenager.

"That's a big responsibility you took on," I stressed. "It proves that you're willing to take charge of things. That's what a businessman or anyone who is successful in life does. You've already shown that you have it within you to be a leader."

Another common denominator of the boys was one of the key things that I had observed so many years ago — why should they follow the rules when the rule makers don't? "And most of you took charge of your life because you hate the hypocrisy of the rule makers," I said to them. "You decided to make your own rules and to follow them faithfully. Of course your rules didn't make the law too happy and that's why you're here. Now, consider this. If you hate hypocrisy, why be part of it? Why change the rules? That's just a cop out to give yourself an excuse. The most effective way to counter the hypocrites is to refuse to break the rules, and to expose them for what they are."

Our discussion of women was particularly memorable. "What do you think about the main character, Dagny Taggert, running a railroad and being a far stronger character than her wimpy brother who's president of the company?" Their initial reaction was laughter and the general consensus was that Rand had given Dagny an unrealistic role. Their girlfriends did what they said after all, and certainly took orders rather than giving them.

"What about your Mom?" I asked. "Does she take orders or give them? I want each of you to answer."

Every boy's answer was the same, and it came most emphatically from the two black youths. I knew the answer from my teen years in Delaware. All of my black friends respected their mother and regarded her as a symbol of strength, not weakness and subservience. Both black teenagers seated at the table confirmed that the role of the black woman in a black family had not changed. The Latino boys indicated that the same was true of their mothers. As I had grown to manhood, I had read and understood that most black families are dominated by a strong woman of high moral values. My wife and I had discussed this with some of our close black friends in Pasadena whose moral strength was our common bond. I made my point with the boys and they conceded that a strong woman could indeed run a railroad.

Another point I made to these boys was the age-old conflict between creators and power seekers. This conflict is present in virtually every chapter of *Atlas Shrugged*. I wanted all of these teenagers to understand the nature of the conflict and to orient his life to that of a creator. I cited numerous examples in the book of the people Rand refers to as "second raters" who seek power, using any ruthless methods they deem necessary.

"For a power seeker, it's really a matter of getting something he hasn't earned. The worst kind of power seeker does it for

EPILOGUE

the sake of destroying a man or woman who is their superior. The creator creates, the power seeker destroys. There are a lot of power seekers involved in politics, and I've seen some of them in action, even experienced their wrath. Ayn Rand identified their nature by saying, 'power-lust is a weed that grows only in the vacant lots of an abandoned mind.' Be forewarned, reality has a way of eventually bringing destruction to those who take pleasure in destroying others. It's the price of not following the Golden Rule."

My message was working. Staff members at Camp Scudder confided to me that some of the boys had asked when I would be back again. I was right in what I had told Rogan. It wasn't a lot different from teaching in a classroom. I really enjoyed meeting with these boys.

———— • ————

I eventually decided to run for the California State Assembly. Outspent by $140,000 to $32,000 I didn't quite make it past the March 2004 Republican primary election. I made a respectable showing however, receiving 47% of the vote.

To protect myself from slander and libel during my campaign for the Assembly, I contacted a friend, Clif Smith, who owns the *San Marino Tribune*, a local paper distributed to cities all over the Pasadena area. We met in his Los Angeles office and I told him what had happened to me in Delaware. I also told him about my work with the boys at Camp Kenyon Scudder.

"Dave, I want you to substantiate everything you've told me," Clif said when I finished. "I want to see the pardon, copies of your SAT scores, your degrees from MIT and Caltech and correspondence between Governor Terry and Mrs. du Pont. Once you send me these documents, I'll write the best story I've ever written."

Clif Smith was true to his word. On December 18, 2003, he published the following column in the *San Marino Tribune*.

Walking in the Shadows of the Past; Seeing the Bright Sun of Tomorrow

La Canada Flintridge. Christmas is a time when people focus on the spirit of giving and helping others. For some, the spirit comes from Christmas itself. For others, the spirit has a different source. Charles Dickens tore readers' hearts when he had his fictional pre-redemption Scrooge dismiss the poor with the famous lines, "Are there no prisons? Are there no workhouses? Better they die and decrease the surplus population." For this one time a year, even television likes to stop shooting at us and blowing up buildings to tell inspirational stories filled with generosity and the spirit of giving. Sometimes we even find a true story among them. This is a true story.

Dave Wilcox believes in helping troubled young people. Every other week, he makes the long drive from his La Canada home to L.A. County's Camp Kenyon Scudder correctional facility to tutor inmates in reading skills. More than that, he exhorts them to believe in themselves, to achieve, to set higher goals for themselves than society is willing to concede them. Wilcox refuses to let them sell themselves short. He believes in them. His belief is almost obsessive and it is contagious.

He's had an impact. Last week, Camp Scudder honored Wilcox at its third annual Sponsors' Appreciation Dinner. So far, Wilcox has taught over a dozen boys and young men and helped them escape a life of imprisonment.

What makes a successful aerospace executive give up a morning week after week to help boys he's never met before and will not likely see again? Wilcox, with degrees from M.I.T. and Cal Tech, really doesn't want to give you an answer. If you persist, really persist, he will tell you very reluctantly and with great humility. Every man has something in his life that inspires him. Often it's a philosophy. For others, it's their faith. It can be someone out of history. More often, though, it's a real person. For Dave Wilcox, his inspiration is a real person he knew many, many years ago — a real-life story of tragedy, destruction, redemption and hope.

Wilcox will tell you about a teenage boy in Delaware who came from a broken home, whose ex-alcoholic father died when the boy was only 14 leaving the son with an embittered mother. Wilcox will tell you about how that boy ran out of control, breaking into cars, burglarizing gas stations, getting arrested, convicted, and sentenced to Delaware state prison for two years. As he tells of this young boy, Wilcox's eyes will cloud with tears and emotion. They are like the tears the boy cried when his lawyer told him that the State of Delaware had no interest in rehabilitating him, but only wanted him locked up to protect everybody else. The boy was only 17 when he was sentenced, around the same age as many boys Wilcox teaches at Camp Scudder. Wilcox remembers the boy and he remembers what the boy did next.

It's what the boy did next that makes Dave Wilcox drive from La Canada to Saugus to help other boys. The boy's story would inspire anyone, and it inspired Dave Wilcox.

This young boy, for whom society had no use, completed the 10th and 11th grades in prison via correspondence courses. He taught himself second year algebra, plane and solid geometry, trigonometry, physics, biology, English, and humanities. The authorities paroled him after one year of the two year sentence. He finished high school and scored a perfect 800 on the SAT math achievement test, today called the SAT II. Still, the boy had a record and was a convicted felon. True, none of the crimes were violent and they were all committed before he was 17, but he was still a convict. That changed, too.

The boy had a patron with one of the most famous names in the country's history and first among Delaware families — Mrs. E. Paul du Pont. She helped many young inmates in the Delaware correctional system who wanted to change.

That was her calling. This boy was one of many. She paid for the boy's education and did even more. One day she took his case to the same man who, as a judge, had sentenced the boy to prison. That man was now the governor of Delaware. The boy's judge and now governor granted him a full pardon wiping out his conviction and cleaning away the stain the boy felt so keenly and with such shame. In pardoning the boy, the governor sentenced him to a lifetime of good behavior, achievement, and good works. Delaware Governor Charles L. Terry, Jr., wrote Mrs. du Pont on May 19, 1966, "It was indeed a pleasure for me to permit this young man to pursue a full and honorable life without a blemish on his record. I believe that his debt to society has been paid." Governor Terry may have called the boy's debt "paid." Dave Wilcox did not.

After receiving his pardon, Dave Wilcox entered M.I.T. and finished in three years. He graduated June 12, 1966 with a bachelor's degree in aeronautics and astronautics. He later was accepted to Cal Tech and earned his Ph.D. in 1970.

He took his degrees and his love for mathematics and science and launched his own company before he was thirty years old. He and his wife of 39 years have two children and two grandchildren. The boy who inspired Dave Wilcox has fulfilled his sentence as a man and he makes that drive to Saugus to help and inspire others. Wilcox is determined to carry out his sentence of a lifetime of good behavior and good works that he gave himself so very, very long ago.

EPILOGUE

When Camp Scudder thanked Dave Wilcox last week, all Wilcox could do was to thank that young boy who, nearly forty years earlier, changed his life. Now, Wilcox makes sure that every troubled boy he meets has the same chance he had to live a life of good behavior, achievement, and good works. So far, so good.

Figure 7.4: *Los Angeles County Supervisor Mike Antonovich presenting me with a commendation for my work at Camp Kenyon Scudder on February 17, 2004.*

The editorial got the attention of the Los Angeles County Probation Department that administers Camp Scudder. The Probation Department was so pleased with my volunteer work that they encouraged Los Angeles County Supervisor Mike Antonovich to officially commend me for my work with the boys. He agreed, and arranged for me to appear at the County Supervisors' meeting on February 17, 2004. All five Supervisors signed the commendation — getting all five signatures is a rare event usually reserved for people with many years of public service.

When you complete this book, you will have read and understood the entire United States Constitution!

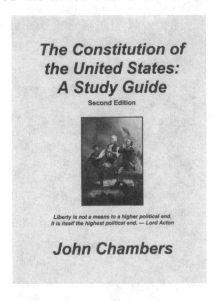

ISBN 1-928729-30-3, 120 pages

This excellent study guide makes teaching and/or understanding the United States Constitution a breeze. It is ideal for a high school course dealing with the essence of America's republican form of government, or for personal study. Author John Chambers points out that it is possible to view the Constitution (or anything) from many different angles — to look at something, one must take a point of view. At the beginning of America's existence as a nation, Alexander Hamilton worked for a strong central government while Thomas Jefferson considered individual liberties to be more important. John Chambers argues that it is the balance of strong central government versus individual liberties, which underlies all Constitutional issues. In presenting the Constitution, he has viewed it from the angle of this balancing act. From that angle, Chambers strives to help you gain a better understanding.

EPILOGUE

If you want to understand the real meaning of the political slogans that permeate America's "drive-by media," this book is a must read.

ISBN 1-928729-00-2, 162 pages

This small monograph is an often humorous and always insightful discussion and analysis of the trite phrases that pass for political discourse in today's America. The book consists of 10 essays focusing on political philosophy, economics and individual liberty. The book has received accolades from respected writers...

- **Milton Friedman, Hoover Institute:** "Clichés of Liberalism is a very well-written, very effective, and persuasive book."
- **R. Emmett Tyrrell, Jr., The American Spectator:** "This is a splendid book that abounds with good sense."

For other educational books, please visit DCW Industries' Home Page . . .